Simon Somerville Laurie

Notes Expository and Critical on Certain British Theories of Morals

Simon Somerville Laurie

Notes Expository and Critical on Certain British Theories of Morals

ISBN/EAN: 9783337338367

Printed in Europe, USA, Canada, Australia, Japan

Cover: Foto ©ninafisch / pixelio.de

More available books at **www.hansebooks.com**

NOTES

EXPOSITORY AND CRITICAL

ON

CERTAIN BRITISH THEORIES OF MORALS.

By SIMON S. LAURIE, A.M.,

AUTHOR OF 'PHILOSOPHY OF ETHICS,' ETC.

EDINBURGH:
EDMONSTON & DOUGLAS.
1868.

CONTENTS.

	PAGE
THOMAS HOBBES,	1
LORD SHAFTESBURY,	7
FRANCIS HUTCHESON,	25
BISHOP BUTLER,	54
TRANSITION.—DAVID HUME,	72
JEREMY BENTHAM,	77
JOHN STUART MILL,	98
PROFESSOR BAIN,	128

PREFACE.

THESE *contributions to the history of ethical speculation in Britain would have had a place in a treatise on the* Philosophy of Ethics, *published by me nearly two years ago, had I not found that an adequate treatment of the various representative writers on Morals involved too great a departure from the line of argument within which I then wished to confine myself.*[1]

Ethical language has undergone so much change from time to time, and has at all times been so loosely employed, that a consistent exposition of the older writers is difficult, and to some extent involves interpretation. If the expositions given in this book

[1] *See footnote to page* 139 *of* Philosophy of Ethics.

are faithful, and if the language of the past is brought into harmony with our present terminology, some service will have been rendered to the student, even should the criticisms be found to fall short of the importance of their several subjects.

S. S. L.

Edinburgh, 1868.

THOMAS HOBBES.

IT is not my purpose either to expound or criticise the ethical system of the philosopher of Malmesbury. The following extracts from his Leviathan and Human Nature—passages which I had marked in the course of my reading—are strung together that the student may have before him some of those moral opinions and definitions which, by their boldness, their vigour, and their consistency, startled the ethical consciousness of England, and formed the point of departure of British Moral speculation, A.D. 1645-1650.

'Whatever is the object of any man's appetite or desire, that is it which he, for his part, calleth *good;* and the object of his hate and aversion, *evil;* and of his contempt, *vile* and *inconsiderable.* For these words of good, evil, and contemptible, are ever used with relation to the person that useth them; there being nothing simply and absolutely so, nor any common rule of good and evil to be taken from the nature of the objects themselves; but from the person of the man where there is no commonwealth, or in a commonwealth from the person that representeth it; or from an arbitrator or judge whom men disagreeing shall by consent set up and make his sentence the rule thereof.'

'*Sudden Glory* is the passion which maketh those *grimaces* called *Laughter;* and is caused either by some sudden act of their own that pleaseth them, or by the apprehension of some deformed thing in another, by comparison whereof they suddenly applaud themselves.'

'*Grief* for the calamity of another is Pity; and riseth from the imagination that a like calamity may befal himself; and therefore is called also Compassion, and, in the phrase of this present time, a fellow-feeling; and, therefore, for calamity arising from great wickedness the best men have the least pity; and for the same calamity those hate pity that think themselves least obnoxious to the same.'

'The acknowledgment of power is called Honour.'

'*Reverence* is the conception we have concerning another, that he hath the *power* to do unto us both *good* and *hurt*, but *not* the *will* to do us *hurt*.'

'*Repentance* is the passion which proceedeth from *opinion* or knowledge that the *action* they have done is *out of the way* to the *end* they would attain: the effect whereof is, to pursue that way no longer, but, by the consideration of the end, to direct themselves into a better.'

'There is yet another passion, sometimes called *Love*, but more properly *Good-will* or charity. There be no greater argument to a man, of his own power, than to find himself able not only to accomplish his own desires, but also to *assist* other men in theirs: and this is that conception wherein consisteth *charity*. In which, first, is contained that *natural affection* of parents to their children, which the Greeks call Στοργὴ, as also, that affection wherewith men seek to *assist* those that adhere unto them. But the affection wherewith men many times bestow their benefits on *strangers*, is not to be called Charity, but either *contract*, whereby they seek to purchase friendship; or fear, which maketh them to purchase peace.'

The 'alternate succession of appetites, aversions, hopes, and fears is no less in other living creatures than in man; and therefore beasts also deliberate.' ... 'In *deliberation* the last appetite or aversion immediately adhering to the action, or to the omission thereof, is that we call the *Will*—the act, not the faculty of willing. And beasts that have *deliberation* must necessarily also have *will*.' ... '*Will, therefore, is the last appetite in deliberating.*'

'Nature hath made men so equal in the faculties of the body and mind, as that though there be found one man sometimes manifestly stronger in body, or of quicker mind than another, yet when all is reckoned together the difference between man and man is not so considerable as that one man can therefore claim to himself any benefit to which another may not pretend as well as he.'

'From this equality of ability ariseth equality of hope in the attaining of our ends. And, therefore, if any two men desire the same thing, which nevertheless they cannot both enjoy, they become enemies; and in the way to their end, which is principally their own conservation, and sometimes their delectation only, endeavour to destroy or subdue one another.'

'So that in the nature of man we find three principal causes of quarrel. First, Competition; second, Diffidence; thirdly, Glory.' ... 'Hereby it is manifest that, during the time men live without a common power to keep them all in awe, they are in that condition which is called War; and such a War as is of every man against every man.'

'The desires and other passions of man are in themselves no sin. No more are the actions that proceed from those passions, till they know a Law that forbids them; which, till laws be made, they cannot know; nor can any law be made till they have agreed upon the person that shall make it.'

'To this war of every man against every man this also is consequent, that nothing can be unjust. The notions of Right and Wrong, Justice and Injustice, have there no place. Where there is no common power there is no Law; where no Law, no injustice.'

Hobbes then deduces nineteen 'Laws of Nature'—a Law of Nature being a 'precept or general rule found out by Reason, by which a man is forbidden to do that which is destructive of his life, or taketh away the means of preserving the same, and to omit that whereby he thinketh it may be best preserved. Among these laws are included all the virtues.

'And the science of these laws is the true and

only Moral Philosophy. For Moral Philosophy is nothing else but the science of what is *good* and *evil* in the conversation and society of mankind. *Good* and *Evil* are names that signify our appetites and aversions; which in different tempers, customs, and doctrines of men are different; and divers men differ not only in their judgment on the senses of what is pleasant and unpleasant to the taste, smell, hearing, touch, and sight, but also of what is unfavourable or disagreeable to reason in the actions of common life. Nay, the same man in divers times differs from himself; and one time praiseth, that is, calleth Good, what another time he dispraiseth and calleth Evil; from whence arise disputes, controversies, and at last war. And, therefore, so long as a man is in the condition of mere nature, which is a condition of war, private appetite is the measure of good and evil; and consequently all men agree on this, that peace is good, and therefore also the way or means of peace, which, as I have showed before, are *justice, gratitude, modesty, equity, mercy,* and the rest of the laws of nature are Good, that is to say, *moral virtues;* and their contrary vices *Evil.* Now the science of Virtue and Vice is Moral Philosophy, and therefore the true doctrine of the laws of nature is the true Moral Philosophy. But the writers of Moral Philosophy, though they acknowledge the same virtues and vices, yet, not seeing wherein consisted their goodness, nor that they come to be praised as the means of peaceable, sociable, and comfortable living, place them in a mediocrity of passions; as if not the cause but the degree of daring made fortitude; or not the cause but the quantity of a gift made liberality. These dictates of reason men used to call by the name of laws, but improperly; for they are but conclusions or theorems concerning what conduceth to the conservation and defence of themselves; whereas Law properly is the word of him that by right hath command over others. But yet, if we consider the same theorems as delivered in the Word of God that by right commandeth all things, then are they properly called Laws.'

Cumberland and Cudworth were the chief opponents of Hobbism. Their speculations, and those of a few writers of less note, fill up the remainder of the 17th century. In 1699 appeared Lord Shaftesbury's *Inquiry concerning Virtue*, which forms the groundwork of all ethical speculations, since that period, on the intuitional side.

THE MORAL THEORY OF LORD SHAFTESBURY.

The connexion between Virtue and Religion is the ostensible subject of Lord Shaftesbury's inquiries. But to show the independence of Virtue on the belief in a God, and on the other hand the dependence of the perfection of it on a *right* conception of the Deity, was impossible without inquiring what Virtue was in itself. Thus his treatise became almost purely ethical. The introductory dissertation on Theism, Atheism, Polytheism, and Dæmonism concludes thus :—'Now, since there are these several opinions concerning a superior Power; and since there may be found perhaps some persons who have no formed opinion at all on this subject, either through scepticism, negligence of thought or confusion of judgment; the consideration is how any of these opinions, or the want of any certain opinion, may possibly consist with virtue and merit, or be compatible with an honest or moral character.'

In prosecuting this inquiry, Shaftesbury begins by considering the end of sensible creatures, as that is revealed by their Constitution or 'Frame.' From this Constitution it appears that each creature has for itself a *private good* and interest, which is a *right* state of that creature, and which is forwarded by nature, and 'affectionately sought' by the creature itself. If anything in the appetites or passions of the creature do not conduce to this end, this private good, it is '*ill*' to him. Further, if the natural constitution is such that by being ill to others he is ill to himself, and by being good to others he is good to himself; and if the being good to others is Virtue, then Virtue and Private Interest agree. That this is the fact will be proved further on. Meanwhile, the prior question, 'What *Goodness* or *Virtue* is?' has to be answered.

If a creature existed such that it was absolutely complete in itself, and sufficient to itself, and had no relation to any other creature or system in the universe of things, it might in a certain sense be called 'Good.' But if it had a relation to a system—if there were something in it which pointed beyond itself,—if it were in truth only a *part* of a whole, and not itself a whole, and yet had no affection or activity in the direction of that system or whole, it manifestly could not be called Good. Nay, if it be merely 'insignificant and of no use,' it is faulty or imperfect, and consequently not good. It is also manifest that if a sensible creature acts for the benefit of the 'system' to which he belongs, by force or without 'affection,' he is neither good nor ill; these qualities being predicable of him only when the 'good or ill of the system to which he has relation is the immediate object of some *passion* or *affection* moving him.' A creature, therefore, is good or ill only *through the affections*.

What, then, are the good or natural affections, and what are the ill or unnatural affections?

That amount of regard to private interest which is

not incompatible with a due regard for the system of which it forms a part is 'not ill:' while that regard to private interest which is essential to the good of the whole or the system, is necessary to constitute a creature *good*. But it is not good, in so far as self-affection or any secondary consideration, such, for example, as Fear, is the motive and the end to the pursuit either of private interest or the good of other creatures; but only in so far as the act is prompted by affection for its kind. Accordingly, 'a good creature is such a one as by the natural temper or bent of its affections is carried *primarily* and *immediately*, and not *secondarily* or *accidentally*, to Good, and against Ill.' And an ill creature is just the contrary.

But proceeding from 'what is esteemed mere Goodness, and lies within the reach and capacity of all sensible creatures, to that which is called *Virtue* or *Merit*, and is allowed to Man only,' we find that, in a creature 'capable of forming general notions of things, not only are the outward beings which offer themselves to the sense the objects of the affection; but that the very actions themselves, and the *affections* of Pity, Kindness, Gratitude, and their contraries, being brought into the mind by reflection, become objects and ends. So that, by the means of this reflected sense, there arises another kind of affection directed towards those very affections themselves which have been already felt, and are now become the subject of a new liking or dislike.' Thus certain affections are at once discerned to be good and virtuous, and certain others bad and vicious, just as the outward eye discerns beauty and deformity in the world of sense. These moral distinctions have their foundation in nature, and the discernment of them is natural, and 'from nature alone.'[1] Thus the mind carries about with it 'characters or pictures of manners,' and in presence of these the heart or Moral Sense cannot remain neutral, but constantly takes part with one 'turn of affection,' and one sentiment or another, approving the honest and natural, and disapproving the dishonest and unnatural. The Heart (Moral Sense), discerning what is good and ill towards the system to which the individual belongs, by affecting the just and right, is virtuous, and by affecting the contrary is the contrary. But it is the reflex act of affecting the notion or conception of the good which makes a man virtuous. For if a creature cannot reflect on what he himself does, or sees others do, so as to take notice of the honest and good, and 'make that *notice* or *conception* of honesty and goodness the object of his affection, he has not the character of being virtuous : for thus, and no otherwise, is he capable of having a *sense of Right or Wrong*.' Right and Wrong are not in the act as such, but in the *affection* which prompts the act. A mistake *in a matter of fact*, for example, being 'no cause or sign of ill affection, can be no cause of vice. But a mistake of *right*' (mistakes which are frequently the consequence of certain religious superstitions), 'being

[1] *The Moralists*, p. 415.

the cause of unequal [*i.e.*, unjust, bad] affection, must of necessity be the cause of vicious action in every intelligent or rational being.' Thus far a knowledge of Right and Wrong is essential to Virtue in every man—that is, such a use of Reason as 'is sufficient to secure a right application of the affections.'

Accordingly, with intelligent creatures goodness [goodnesses], virtues, etc., constitute 'rational objects,' and become 'rational affections;' and where these rational affections triumph over the 'sensible' or non-rational, a man is rightly called virtuous. Provided always it be the affection towards Goodness or Virtue which has led to the triumph, and not some secondary motive or ulterior self-interested end.

'The nature of Virtue consisting in a certain just disposition or proportionable affection of a rational creature towards the moral objects of Right and Wrong, nothing can, in such a creature, exclude a principle of virtue, or render it ineffectual, except what either takes away the *natural* and *just* sense of Right and Wrong; or creates a *wrong* sense of it; or causes the right sense to be opposed by *contrary* affections. And again, nothing can advance virtue in a man, except what either nourishes and promotes a sense of Right and Wrong; or preserves it genuine and uncorrupt; or causes it, when such, to be obeyed, by subduing and subjecting the other affections to it.' Shaftesbury then proceeds to consider the possible influence for good or evil in these three directions of the various opinions regarding the Supreme Being, set forth in the beginning of his essay on Virtue. It is unnecessary to follow him through this part of his argument; because although full of suggestive thoughts on a subject of great interest, it has not, in the present state of ethical inquiry, a direct bearing on the leading problems. His concluding words on this topic will therefore suffice :—

'Hence we may determine justly the relation which Virtue has to Piety ; the first being not complete but in the latter ; since where the latter is wanting there can neither be the same benignity, firmness, nor constancy ; the same good composure of the affections or uniformity of mind. And thus the perfection and height of Virtue must be owing to the belief of a God.'

In his second book Shaftesbury, having in the previous part of his treatise considered 'What Virtue is,' and to whom the character of 'Virtuous' properly belongs, enters on the question of the '*Obligation to Virtue.*' In establishing this obligation, he proceeds by first repeating as his starting-point that 'Rectitude, Integrity, or Virtue,' is to have one's affections right and *entire,* not only in respect of one's self, but in respect of the Kind or System of which we form a part. He then combats the opinion that Self-interest is in opposition to the Public interest or good, although the respective affections (Selfish and Good) have objects which seem to imply an inherent antagonism. That the fact is quite the reverse, he shows by citing, by way of illustration, the misery of the ill-humoured, rancorous, and perverse man. With reference to such cases, he shows that we are too apt to omit from our reckoning the balanced constitution of our nature, and the discord and consequent misery which ensues on a disturbance of its harmony. We forget to regard ourselves in the light of the notion of a *Whole* made up of parts, and thus fail to understand how some particular act should result in moral pain. When a man is thoroughly bad, we all admit that he is miserable, while sometimes disposed to doubt the wretchedness which must naturally follow from any one particular vicious act. If we kept in view this 'fabrick' of the mind, we should see that 'whoever did ill, or acted in prejudice of his Integrity, Good-nature, or Worth, would of necessity act with greater cruelty towards himself than he who scrupled not to swallow what was poisonous, or who, with his own hands, should voluntarily mangle or wound his *outward* form or constitution, natural limbs or body.'

Entering more into detail, Shaftesbury goes on to show that the Affections or Passions which may influence or govern are '(1.) The Natural Affections, which lead to the good of the *Public;* (2.) The Self-Affections, which lead only to the good of the *Private;* and (3.) Such as are neither of these, nor tending to any Good of either the Public or Private, but contrariwise; and which therefore may justly be styled unnatural affections.' The last sort is wholly vicious; the two former may be vicious or virtuous, according to their degree. For, it is not right that the Self-affections should be too weak, nor, on the other hand, that the Public affections should be too strong. He recurs here to the idea of an inward constitution or economy, and maintains that virtue is not truly attained where harmony and balance of the passions and affections are lost. If, for example, Self-affections are overpowered by the Public, the whole system suffers, as well as the individual. Strictly speaking, therefore, to have any 'natural affection too high, or any self-affection too low, though it be often approved as a Virtue, is a Vice and Imperfection.' *Strictly speaking* it is so; but at the same time he confesses that a man is properly to be considered as vicious, only when (1.) Either the public affections are weak and deficient; (2.) or the private and self-affections are too strong; or (3.) (as stated above) where such affections arise as tend neither to the support of the public or private system, but contrariwise. His next task is to consider these three mental conditions, with a view to show that it is contrary to man's *interest* to manifest any of these affections, and that it is '*his Interest to be wholly Good and Virtuous.*'

First, it has to be shown that 'to have the natural affections (such as are founded in Love, Complacency, Goodwill, and a sympathy with the Kind or Species) is to have the chief means and power of self-enjoyment; and, that to want them is certain misery and ill.' To prove this, we must first know what it is which constitutes Happiness, which may be summed up as the Pleasures of the Body and the Mind. The Pleasures of the Mind are much greater than those of the Body; and it consequently follows, that whatever creates in any intelligent being a constant flowing series of mental enjoyments, is of more importance to his happiness than bodily pleasures. As such mental enjoyments are either the 'natural' [the good, kindly, virtuous] affections in their *immediate* operation, or proceed from them as their effects, the due establishment of these in a creature is the only means of procuring a certain and solid happiness. Shaftesbury then illustrates this position in detail, by showing the genuine pleasures which are yielded to a rational being by the cultivation of the social and friendly, the Intellectual and the Virtuous (by which he here means consciously exercised benignant), affections; even the very grief of the affections being associated with a deeper pleasure than the satisfaction of our common appetites. With reference to the *effects* of the activity of these affections, he cites the pleasures of participating in the joys of others, and the reflected approbation which comes back to us as the doers of benignant deeds. He then shows that the *partial* exercise of these affections—their grudging exercise—does not result in pleasure, but in the reverse; while the hearty and entire affection (which he identifies with Integrity of mind) carries along with it a consciousness of merited love and approbation from all society, and is truly to 'live according to nature and the dictates and rules of supreme wisdom, is Morality, Justice, Piety, and natural Religion.'

But further, man, by virtue of his reason, is a Reflective Animal, and is capable of self-inspection and self-approbation. This reflective approval or disapproval of the just and natural, or unjust and unnatural, act is properly called *Conscience*—a name not strictly applicable to the approval or disapproval of acts merely prejudicial to our own private interests. This *moral conscience* precedes and presupposes *religious* Conscience. For the fear of the terrors of the Deity does not imply a Conscience at all, except where there is also a self-reprobation of the wrong and ill-deserving act *in itself*. Conscience is 'a sense of deformity in what is ill-deserving and unnatural;' also 'a consequent shame or regret at incurring what is odious and moves aversion.' He also defines it 'a natural sense of the odiousness of crime and injustice.' Now, if the reflex power gives rise in the case of the Vicious to such feelings, they *must* be most miserable. And if it were alleged that there were men without any such moral sense, it would then also follow that they could not be capable of natural affection; and 'if not of that, then neither of any social pleasure or mental enjoyment,' or of their effects, as these have been expounded above. As to that other kind of conscience not strictly so called—the reflection on 'what was at any time unreasonably and foolishly done in prejudice of one's real interest or happiness' [*i.e.*, *private* or self-interest as opposed to the natural and virtuous affections]—Shaftesbury points to the indirect effect on such private good of a want of those affections, which bring in their train the approbation and reciprocated kindness of our fellow-men, summing up thus :—

'From all this we may easily conclude how much our happiness depends on natural and good affection. For if the chief happiness be from the Mental Pleasures, and the chief Mental Pleasures are such as we have described, and are founded in natural affection, it follows that to have the natural affections is to have the chief means and power of Self-enjoyment, the highest possession and Happiness of life.'

Shaftesbury then endeavours to show that even the pleasures of Sense are satisfactions only to the extent to which they imply social and natural affection ; and passes finally to the consideration of that inner balance which nature intended as its end, wherever it gave a *Constitution* or *Economy*, and to which reference had several times been made in the course of his general exposition. In this inward Constitution we find given natural and public as well as private affections ; and that constitution consequently suffers and is impaired wherever due activity is denied to these affections ; nay, they will force their prison-house, and create for themselves 'unusual and unnatural,' and therefore destructive exercise. 'Whoever is the least versed in this moral kind of architecture, will find the inward fabrick so adjusted, and the *whole* so nicely built, that the barely extending of a single passion a little too far, or the continuance of it too long, is able to bring irrecoverable ruin and misery.'

'Thus we have demonstrated that to have the natural and good affections is to have the chief means and power of self-enjoyment: So, on the other side, to want them is certain misery and ill.'

Shaftesbury now goes on to prove that, by 'having the *Self*-passions too intense or strong, a creature becomes miserable.' These Self or 'Home' affections (as he calls them) are Love of Life; Resentment of Injury; Pleasure or Appetite towards nourishment and the means of generation; Interest, or the desire of those conveniences by which we are well provided for and maintained; Emulation or Love of Praise and Honour; Indolence, or Love of Ease and Rest. These, taken together, constitute, according to Shaftesbury, Interestedness or Self-Love.

That the excess of these self-affections is injurious to the *Public* Interest, all admit; that they are also injurious to the private interest of the individual who indulges them, may easily be proved. It is unnecessary for us here to follow Shaftesbury. If the names which he gives to the excess of these passions are accepted, viz., Cowardice, Revengefulness, Luxury, Avarice, Vanity and Ambition, and Sloth, we may spare ourselves the trouble of showing that they are evils to the individual no less than to society—evils in themselves, as well as by losing us our natural affections, on which we have shown the happiness of man mainly to depend.

The next step in the argument is to show that those passions which contribute to the advancement neither of the public nor private system, or which are *unnatural*, tend to the misery of the individual agent. To name them is enough : for who can doubt that Inhumanity, Petulancy (wanton mischievousness), Malignity, Envy, Misanthropy, Superstition, Lusts, Tyranny, Ingratitude, where they possess the human soul, cause Misery 'in the highest degree?'

From all which argument we are driven to the conclusion that to be wicked or vicious is to be miserable and unhappy—is, in other words, to injure Self. On the other hand, it is equally manifest that the Happiness and Good of Virtue, and *therefore* also its obligation, are beyond question. If further evidence were needed, it would be found in what we have stated respecting the Balance and Economy of our inner nature.

Thus, then, 'the Wisdom of what rules and is First and Chief in Nature has made it to be according to the private interest and good of every one to work towards the general good; which, if a creature ceases to promote, he is actually so far wanting to himself, and ceases to promote his own happiness and welfare. He is on this account directly his own enemy, nor can he any otherwise be good and useful to himself than as he continues good to society, and to that whole of which he is himself a part. So that Virtue, which of all excellences and beauties is the chief and most amiable; *that* which is the prop and ornament of human affairs; which upholds communities, maintains union, friendship, and correspondence amongst men; *that* by which countries as well as private families flourish and are happy, and for want of which everything comely, conspicuous, great, and worthy must perish and go to ruin; *that single quality*, thus beneficial to all society and to mankind in general, is found equally a happiness and good to each creature *in particular*, and is that by which alone man can be happy, and without which he must be miserable. And this Virtue is the Good, and Vice is the Ill of every one.'[1]

With Shaftesbury, words which are now distinguished, and many of which had been distinguished by Hobbes, are used as synonymous; sometimes they are interchanged in senses not strictly equivalent. Hence it is requisite to seize the main line and final purpose of his thought, as we have endeavoured to do, if we would interpret him in the sense which he himself would have accepted. Looking at his system in

[1] It may not be superfluous here to point out that our exposition and criticism have reference only to the moral *theories*, not the moral writings, of Shaftesbury and others. Were it otherwise, it would be impossible to omit an account of 'The Moralists' of which Leibnitz wrote with such generous enthusiasm, recognising in it the substance of his *Théodicée*.

this liberal and sympathetic spirit, we are able to discern in it the basis of all the Intuitionalism of the eighteenth century. Virtue, Merit, Worth, Right consist, according to him, in the exhibition of the *natural* affections, by which he means those affections which have for their object the good of our kind, that is, of the rational system of which we form a part. This Virtue is further seen to be the End of man's constitution, as soon as we have learned that man is an 'Economy,' a Whole made up of parts. Self-interest, meanwhile, under which we may include all those desires and acts which have for their ultimate end the satisfaction of the individual, is legitimately the object of our concern, provided it be subject to the controlling influence of the natural or public affections. Where these latter, however, do not directly or indirectly enter, there is no Virtue, no Merit, no Worth. The defect of Shaftesbury's theory is not to be found in his conception of the end of man, but in the limited notion which he forms of Virtue, which is the condition of man's attaining his end. Virtue has a much wider range than he concedes to it: it embraces the notion of Moral Law, and obedience to it as such; and it also embraces those Self-regarding Moral ends which do not in their intent touch the Public good; which, in truth, derive their distinctive moral character from the fact that they exalt the personality of the agent. The very word *integrity* has to him no meaning except that of *entirety of public affection*. He also errs in assuming throughout as a postulate that the *aggregate* of Happiness is the end of man, failing to distinguish subjective Happiness as a test of action from the sum of Happiness—these two things being in truth most commonly incompatible.

Having determined the end of man, and wherein consists the Right or Virtuous in Action, he only slightly touches on the question of the faculty by which we discriminate this 'Right,' and still more slightly on the authority which belongs to it, and which *constitutes* it 'the Right.' The moment we see exhibited those affections commonly known as virtuous and laudable, we are so constituted, he affirms, that we instantaneously approve them. We have, then, thus far a 'Moral Sense.' With regard to subjective acts, again, such as the preference of mental to bodily pleasures, he appeals to the universal *sense* of all who have experienced both. He does not claim for man any distinct faculty by means of which right purposes and acts are each individually pronounced good, but only a power of reflectively comparing the pleasures, bodily, mental, and moral, which *have been* enjoyed, and, by means of this reflex act, setting one above the other. This reflex act of approbation is Shaftesbury's Conscience or Moral Sense—it is the Sense of the Virtuous, the consciousness of a man with himself that he is Right or Wrong. The doctrine is erroneous, rather by defect than otherwise. Inner authority and Law—the supreme fact of ethical Consciousness is not explained. The path of Virtue is so plain and flowery, that the phenomena of Law, Duty, Struggle, Remorse scarcely enter into the writer's thoughts. They can have no place where all is so beautiful to the moral eye, so seductive, so easy and so advantageous.

The *Obligation* to Virtue, again, is simply the obligation to pursue that which is so conspicuously our only happiness, both when we look to our lower and to our higher interests, that not to pursue it is the extremity of folly. The weakness of this part of his system is sufficiently revealed in the phrase which he employs as an equivalent for obligation to Virtue, viz., *reason to embrace it*. He never for a moment dreams of any obligation other than Self-interest. His system might in many respects be regarded as an extension of the Hobbistic use of that term.

Such a theory of refined Eudæmonism, while containing much well-reasoned truth, has after all proved only this, that Virtuous affections no less than private or self-affections are *natural* to man; that if we cultivate the former, giving free scope to self-interest only to the extent to which it does not conflict with these, we shall be happy; and that *thus only* can we be happy. The test, the ultimate criterion, therefore, of all actions is Happiness—the aggregate Happiness of the individual agent.

That the theory of Morality should be left at this point was impossible. There were deeper things in man's nature than this refined, and cultivated, and well-balanced mind had been able to see. Rose-colour is not the prevailing hue of mortal life. There is an inner discord deep and mysterious; there is a self-end which yet is not a personal end; there is a supreme law which does not lie without; there is a terrible voice of authority in the heart, and a terrible possibility of Remorse. A stronger hand was needed to take up the lamp of thought and carry it into these remote recesses. That hand was the hand of Bishop Butler. But before we discuss the merits and defects of his higher doctrine, we must give a place to another prophet of intuitional eudæmonism, Francis Hutcheson, whose name has been specially identified with the doctrine of a *Moral Sense*.

FRANCIS HUTCHESON (1725).

With full and explicit recognition of his indebtedness to Shaftesbury, Hutcheson entered upon the same field in which his predecessor had achieved so much and so well merited distinction. His original treatise was specially directed against the reasonings of Mandeville,—a circumstance which necessarily modified his course of argument. He differed from his master also in his point of view, and, consequently, in his manner of approaching the question. It was not the existence of the Virtuous affections in man, and the Happiness of Virtue which mainly interested him and which gave stimulus to his thought and balance and closeness to his argument, but the 'Sense' whereby certain mental states were discerned to be virtuous. This question, although not ignored by Shaftesbury, had not been deliberately taken up by him as a central and vital one.

In the preface to the fourth edition of his *Inquiry*,[1] Hutcheson himself tells us that his principal design was 'to show that Human Nature was not left quite indifferent in the affairs of Virtue to form to itself

---

[1] Hutcheson's *Inquiry into the Original of our Ideas of Beauty and Virtue* appeared in 1725. In 1728 he published an *Essay on the Nature and Conduct of the Passions and Affections*, which contained illustrations and extensions of his theory, and very subtle controversion of the theories of Clarke, Woolaston, and others. A fourth edition of his original work was published, with corrections, in 1738. His *Introduction to Moral Philosophy*, and the *Posthumous Lectures*, published (in 1735) after his death, contain also a statement of his theory.

observations concerning the advantage or disadvantage of actions, and accordingly to regulate its conduct,' but that the Almighty had given us strong affections to be the springs of Virtue, and made Virtue herself 'a lovely form, that we might easily distinguish it from its contrary.'

In conducting the inquiry which is to establish this opinion, he begins by stating that Moral Goodness is the Quality in actions which causes us to approve or love the agent, and by asking whence this approbation arises.

Our sensible perceptions yield us pleasure, and those things which directly yield us the pleasures of sense are called *good*, and give origin to the word; while those things which mediately lead to these pleasures are called useful or advantageous. The former are *immediately*, the latter *mediately*, Good. Thus far we discern the influence of Hobbes.

Hence it is apparent that our sense of Pleasure precedes our perception of the Advantageous, and is the foundation of the perception.

When we seek such pleasures or *goods*, e.g., the sensuous and the artistic, or what mediately leads to them, Riches, we seek them from *Interest* or *Self-Love*.

Many hold that those actions and dispositions which we call Moral are *obeyed* by us because they are the *Laws* of a Superior Being, and, as Law, carry with them rewards and punishments of a general kind, which make it our Self-Interest to obey them; and that in so far as we *approve* them in others, we do so because we see their bearing on the *natural good* of the whole, and therefore to some extent on our own. The ground of approbation, as well as the motive of morality, is thus reduced to Self-interest, or regard to selfish pleasures distinct from the mere moral act as such. Virtue is thus a mediate, not an immediate, Good.

Others hold that we are by our nature determined to a sense or perception of pleasure, or of *immediate* good or beauty, in certain acts and dispositions *as such*, whether in others or ourselves, apart from any consequent advantage; but that our motive in performing such actions is merely the realizing in ourselves of that pleasurable sensation just as we seek after fine landscapes or statues in order to gratify our sense of beauty: and thus they reduce motives of action to *Self-Interest* in another form—only substituting, in point of fact, the immediate for the mediate.

Hutcheson's object is to show—

' I. That some actions have to men an *immediate* goodness, or that by a *Superior Sense*, which he calls a Moral one, we approve the actions of others, and perceive them to be their perfection and dignity, and are determined to love the agent. A like perception we have in reflecting on such actions of our own, without any view of *natural* advantage from them.

' II. That the Affection, Desire, or Intention which gains approbation to the actions flowing from it, is not an intention to obtain even this *sensible pleasure*, much less the future rewards from sanctions of laws or any other *natural good* which may be the consequence of the virtuous action, but an entirely different principle of action from Self-Love or Desire of Private Good.'

The course of argument runs thus :—
Had we no Sense or instinctive feeling of Good distinct from advantage, interest, or 'natural good' (all which terms are, with Hutcheson, synonymous), we should have the same *kind* of pleasurable feeling towards a commodious house that we have towards a generous or noble character. So with Evil and the incommodious. Hence it is evident that there is an instinctive feeling of Good on the presentation of certain acts, which we separate from others as *Moral*. In other words, there is a Moral Sense which, as an inner determination, corresponds to those outer determinations, the external senses ; by which external senses we mean, he says, '*a Determination of the Mind to receive any idea from the presence of an object which occurs to us, independently of our Will.*'

To say that our pleasure in the moral qualities of those great actions which adorn the past, arises from our perceiving that they might have been advantageous to us had we lived in the time and place of their performance, is untrue in fact ; for did our advantage, interest, or natural good determine our feeling, the successful tyrant would engage our affection, not unsuccessful virtue.

But it may be maintained that our perception of the beautiful and good, in actions not directly affecting our own 'natural good,' arises from the fact that we know that whatever profits one part profits the whole, and thus some small share may ultimately reach each individual; and that actions which contemplate the good of the whole, if universally performed, would most effectually secure the good of each individual, and of ourselves among others. To this the answer is, that there is no such reflection on the effect of acts, and that our approbation is immediate. We admire more the act of Codrus than that of the miser who buried a pot of gold which we may have found, and who has thus contributed much more to our personal *advantage* than the former did. Further, it will be found that although our *Desire* of Virtue in ourselves or others may be counterbalanced by *Interest*, our sentiment or perception of its beauty and of the deformity of the opposite cannot be influenced in this way.

Accordingly we conclude that we have in us a *Moral Sense* directing our actions—by which is meant not any *innate idea* or *practical proposition*, but a 'Determination of our minds to receive the simple ideas of Approbation or Condemnation, from actions observed, antecedently to any opinions of advantage or loss to redound to ourselves from them, even as we are pleased with a regular Form or harmonious

Composition' in itself, and apart from advantage or disadvantage.

Having shown that there is a *Moral Sense,*—that is, an inner determination of Feeling, whereby one action performed by others or by ourselves is immediately, and without reference to any other considerations whatsoever, felt to be beautiful or virtuous and another deformed or vicious, Hutcheson next proceeds to consider the Motive which impels to virtuous acts.

The proposition which he now endeavours to prove is, that every action which is morally good or evil is supposed to flow from some affection towards *rational agents,* that is, towards God or Man ; and that the moment we separate an act from such presumed affection it loses its moral character. *Temperance,* for example, except in so far as it arises from obedience to God, is not morally good, but simply an attention to *natural* good, viz., health. *Courage,* except when stimulated by love of country or hatred of wrong, is not a virtue. So with *Prudence* (if it regards only *individual* interest) and *Justice.*

Hutcheson then argues thus : Virtue consists in certain *Affections,* or actions consequent on these affections ; and if it can be shown that these affections do not spring from self-love or self-interest, it will appear that 'Virtue is not pursued from any regard to the interest or self-love of the pursuer.' All affections are but modifications of Love and Hate. The former is subdivided into Love of (*i.e.,* which consists in) Complacence or Esteem, and Love of (*i.e.*, which consists in) Benevolence. Now, both these affections are stirred in us immediately by the presentation of certain qualities in objects, which qualities we *must* love. No appeal to our *advantage* in respect of 'natural' goods would induce us to the active exercise of esteem or benevolence, although it might induce us to simulate these affections. We conclude that self-interest, in none of its forms, can lead us to that love of others which is expressed by Esteem and Benevolence in their various modifications, and that the originating cause of these affections in us is a *generous Instinct*, which comes into operation on the presentation of its objects, and which has nothing to do with our self-love, or interest, or advantage, or natural good, but only with itself and its object.

If this be the case with Esteem or Benevolence, it is equally so with other virtuous affections, such as Fear or Reverence in presence of Goodness, Power, and Justice. Were it possible to have these affections towards a being simply from regard to the effect on our interests, we could be *bribed* to entertain them towards a being not good, which is by our nature impossible. Here again, therefore, it appears that all virtue flows from love to *Persons*, or some other affection equally *disinterested;* and that, when we are excited to virtuous actions, we are so from some other motive than self-interest, just as when we *feel* the virtue of actions this feeling has been shown to be independent of self-love or interest in any form.

Now, we come to the question, 'Is Virtue pursued because of the concomitant pleasure?' No, says Hutcheson. For, first, if 'we pursue Virtue because it is pleasant, then before we resolved to pursue it there must have been a *prior* sense of Virtue, antecedent to ideas of advantage' upon which the knowledge of this *advantage* is founded. Secondly, some Virtue or the practising of some virtuous affections, such as Sorrow, Anger, Compassion, is not pleasant. These affections arise, and ought to arise, on the occurrence of the suitable objects; and painful though they be, we could not justify to ourselves the extinction of the affections while the objects which roused them were present. It is not motives of self-love, then, but the frame of our nature which 'determines us to be thus affected, and approves our being so.' In like manner, the pleasant virtuous affections are not chosen by us *because* they are pleasant, but they arise simply on seeing their objects.

True, if we have practised virtuous affections, we may, 'after the passion is over,' have pleasure in *calm reflection*, from the consideration that 'we have been in a disposition which, to our Moral Sense, appears lovely and good: but this pleasure is never intended in the heat of action, nor is it any motive exciting to it.'

Having shown that the loving of virtuous actions proceeds neither from Self-interest on the one side, nor from the Pleasure of Virtue on the other, Hutcheson next proceeds to show that it is '*Some Determination of our nature to study the good of others; or some instinct antecedent to all reason (reasoning) from interest which influences us to the love of others, even as the Moral sense determines us to approve the actions which flow from this love in ourselves or others.*'

This proposition is illustrated by the love of parents for their children. If it be said that the parent suffers when his child suffers, and that *on this account* he is affected with a loving desire to remove the suffering, is not this to say that love to the child *causes* him to suffer with it? If so, then Love is antecedent to any conjunction of interest—the cause, not the effect. Nature, in short, determines us to have affection for him; and if so, why not, though in a weaker form, for all mankind? In truth, where there is no interfering personal interest, we shall find this Love existing towards all rational agents in some degree.

Love of country is itself, *to a great extent,* only love of individuals whom, in various relations, we have seen, as members of the same community with ourselves, manifesting those dispositions which our Moral Sense compels us to approve. When there is an apparent want of natural benevolence, it is because the instinctive inclination is overpowered by Self-interest (or, it ought to be added, by Anger or Displeasure); but where 'this does not happen, we shall find all mankind under its influence, although with different degrees of strength, according to the nearer or more remote relations they stand in to each other.

Before proceeding further, let us take a critical retrospect of the leading features of our author's argument. That man has an inner, instinctive, immediate sense of pleasure or beauty, or by whatever name it may be called, when he becomes cognisant in others or in himself of those dispositions commonly called Virtuous, in the limited sense of Benevolent, we think Hutcheson has demonstrated. It flows from this, that by the inner, instinctive, immediate feeling, man separates the good from the bad in actions, in so far at least as this specific quality is concerned, and discriminates the approvable and the censurable. He has made good his point against both what we would call Utilitarian selfism,—that is, the reduction of the grounds of approvableness, and therefore of Right and Wrong in conduct, to the perception of a mediate or immediate production of 'natural good' to the individual approving; as well as against what might be called Utilitarian universalism, which reduces the grounds of approvableness, and therefore of Right and Wrong, to the perceived tendency of the act to promote the natural good or interests of the community, and so, indirectly, of the individual, as a member of it. He has also shown that this moral liking does not flow from the perception that the acts and dispositions approved originate in the *Law* of a superior being, to be enforced by the increase or decrease of 'natural' pleasures or pains, although this perception doubtless supports, confirms, and intensifies the moral approbation or reprobation.

Our author, in next endeavouring to find the motives of virtuous actions, is anxious to show that these motives are not only not the desire of 'natural' good or self-interest, but not even the *pleasure of Virtue itself*. In his first object he partially succeeds, in the second he fails. The fact that he only partially succeeds in the one case and entirely fails in the other, is due to an insufficient analysis of human nature and the ends of action, and of the character of moral energizing.

As we have seen in the above statement of his system, he considers no acts moral or virtuous save those which are prompted by an affection for *rational agents*. This is to identify the moral with those acts and dispositions only which are *transitive*,—and not only so, but which are purposely transitive. His manifest failure to force into this category the virtues of temperance, under which would be included, we presume, chastity and purity, as well as general self-control, courage, under which would fall self-sacrifice of the body for the sake of the truth apart from affection towards God, and prudence with its manifold subspecies, not to speak of virtues altogether ignored by him, such as integrity, dignity, and magnanimity, which have regard to self alone, and are not affections toward other Rational agents,—is sufficient evidence that he has rashly committed himself to a general conclusion regarding the nature of Virtue before undertaking a sufficiently broad inquiry into the specific ends of action and the Supreme end of all. Had he separated the Intransitive from the Transitive ends, he would have been driven from the position which he took up, and which compelled him to merge all virtue, all morality, in Love to mankind, or (as in the case of the virtues of reverence, etc.) Love to God.

This mode of accounting for the motives which impel to virtuous conduct reacts, it will be at once seen, on the theory of a Moral Sense, by reducing the action and range of that sense simply to a feeling of immediate pleasure at discerning Love in others towards Rational agents. It would follow that all those virtues falling under the general names Prudence, Integrity, Purity, must be discriminated as approvable on other grounds; that is, not immediately by a sense, but mediately by the understanding. From this a conclusion would follow, which Hutcheson would have himself strongly deprecated, namely, that these virtues are approved not in themselves, but because they promote our lower interests, *or* the lower interests of others.[1]

Further, to say that we do not pursue virtue for the sake of the pleasure of Virtue, because to do so itself presupposes a 'Sense of Virtue antecedent to ideas of advantage,' is to employ the word 'advantage' in a

---

[1] It may be observed, in passing, that virtues may be displayed in relation to irrational agents as well as to rational.

connexion in which it has no proper significance. This word has been generally used by Hutcheson as synonymous with 'promotive of some natural good or lower interest other than the affection, or sentiment, or what not, which is *immediately* the object of approbation or of pursuit.' The opinion which Hutcheson attempts to redargue, however, is that the Virtuous disposition or act is *in itself* pleasurable, and desired *because of* the pleasure which it yields to the agent. Hutcheson confounds the history of the origin of the virtuous dispositions (that is to say, of the instinct of benevolence, for, as we have seen, all virtue is, in his opinion, merged in this instinct) with these same dispositions, as elements in the moral conflict, which is always transacting itself in the breast of every man. The virtuous or benevolent affections, it is true, like all the passions, arise only in conjunction with their objects; it is *others as loved*, not the *love* of others, that we first instinctively know; again, it is a supreme and perfect Being reverenced, not the reverence of a supreme and perfect Being, which first comes within the range of our mental experience. But these mental states once experienced, we recognise in ourselves the Love of others, and reverence towards the Supreme as instinctive moral forces working in us, and presenting along with other forces a claim of right in the court of Will. Thus it happens that when the rational will has to act, the *same* object may be to it the external recipient of a selfish, a malignant, a benevolent, a heroic, a pious or an impious act; and the question to be settled is this, with which of these dispositions to act shall I here and now identify my Will, which is myself? These dispositions, primary, instinctive, derivative, simple, or complex, are realities—the objects which I (that is, the Will) am first to seize. But they of necessity carry with them the external objects. It belongs essentially to the *notion* of them that they externalize themselves, and connect self and not-self in a completed act by means of the uniting sentiment. Without this union, the identification of self with the sentiment is not at all accomplished in the region of the moral, but only in the region of knowledge.

Hutcheson, it seems to us, was afraid to recognise the pleasure of virtue as a motive to virtue; because by so doing he would have separated virtuous action from self-interested action only by the *kind* of pleasure which it yielded to the agent. Thus would be laid the foundation of a *personal* eudæmonism which might justify to itself any course of action on the simple ground of idiosyncratic preference. And to this danger, and to a loose theory of obligation and of law, Hutcheson unquestionably did expose himself, notwithstanding his efforts to avoid it.

If we look, again, at his argument from the point of view of the self-reference of Virtue, we shall find that, in endeavouring so eagerly as he does to show that the virtuous or benevolent act does not originate in a desire for the happiness it yields to the agent, but in the love the agent has of the happiness of others, Hutcheson overlooks the distinction between Self-love and Self-interest; and this leads to much confusion of statement and much logomachy. His two leading arguments in refutation of what he believes to be a selfish theory of virtue are—(1.) That the virtuous affection arises in us only on the presentation of the fitting object, and cannot be called into operation by an act of volition merely; that, in short, it is of the nature of an instinct. (2.) That when we do generous offices, we do not *intend* our own happiness but the happiness of others; and that, in truth, the contemplation of our own happiness would destroy the moral or virtuous character of the benevolent act. The answer to the first refutation is that although psychologically Hutcheson is correct, yet it is equally a psychological truth that we can, by an act of will, initiate a movement towards an affection or sentiment as an object. The answer to the second is, that in seeking the good of others, we, by his own showing, do really seek our own highest felicity—the indulgence of the *love* of the good of others; and this without regard to the consequent and retrospective approbation of ourselves for having sought the good of others. Indeed, the fact that we retrospectively *approve* ourselves for benevolent acts, can find in Hutcheson's theory no consistent explanation: self-approbation becomes lost in the instinctive pleasure of the act of loving, and identified with it. Reflection on this might, by bringing to light the ground of approbation, have suggested the true motive to the virtuous act. To separate an act done for the sake of the good of others (apart from any ulterior or lower interest) from a subjective pleasure in the good of others, and in the particular act done, is impossible, except for purposes of thought. I may cultivate in myself a mental condition of *Love* towards my fellow-men, and delude myself by indulging in this mood, and usurping to myself the further pleasure of self-approbation for my virtuous disposition. But in so doing, Benevolence is present to my mind only as an object of knowledge, or it may be that it expends itself on subject-objects purely imaginary. To seek after this pleasure is *not* to cultivate benevolence, but rather, indeed, to weaken it, and to substitute for that virtue a morbid and will-enervating consciousness of the possibility of exercising the virtue. On the other hand, to seek to do good to others from any other motive than a purely moral one, such as the realizing in our consciousness of the pleasure of the benevolent act, is itself also an act without virtue, as Hutcheson himself would admit. In short, there is in man the antagonism of the lower and the higher, self-interest and self-love,—the one strong and powerful, the other lofty and supreme; and when we seek the supreme joy of our nature, we do so at great cost, and by an effort of free rational volition, which constitutes its moral worth, its virtuous character, and its disinterestedness. That, in certain classes of action, the good of others should be precisely the quality which yields the Agent a supreme felicity; that we cannot contemplate the object of our activity as happy, save in and through the subject as happy, and *vice versa;* that, in short, the subjective end and the objective end concur and are inseparable, does not touch the morality or virtue of the active desire, or of the election of it by the will as a motive force.

Having discussed the subjects of a Moral Sense and the Motives to Virtuous action, Hutcheson next proceeds to inquire what common quality is found to be the essential characteristic of all those acts which are approved by the Moral Sense. The answer, viz., *Benevolence* or *Love*—has been already given in the course of discussing prior questions.

When this doctrine has to be applied to the worship and fear of God, it breaks down, in our opinion, by omitting from view the morality which resides in the mere act of submission to a recognised superior. The effort made to make this a case of love contradicts history and the facts of human nature.

Especially forced is the attempt to reduce those virtues which are usually referred to enlightened Self-Love to acts into which benevolence enters, and must enter, in order to constitute them *moral.* For example, he says that since the individual is a part of the whole, a due regard to himself is thus far a regard for the whole, even where the good of the whole is not contemplated. Not only so ; a want of due self love would be universally pernicious, and self-love within limits prescribed by the universal good is, *therefore*, moral and approvable. This is a violent attempt to justify his reduction of all virtue to benevolence.

In other parts of his writings, Hutcheson occasionally extends the operation of the Moral Sense to those powers and dispositions which have to do with the moral perfection of the mind possessing them, and we consequently expect to find it brought to bear on those *intransitive* acts which constitute so large a part of the virtuous character. But he quickly loses sight of this relation of the Moral Sense, and characteristically confines its activity to the detection of benevolence in all good affections of whatsoever kind. In so far as it detects this quality it *approves* them; in so far as it finds it wanting it is indifferent; in so far as it finds it contravened it condemns.[1] Even veracity, candour, fortitude, and so forth, although they '*seem* to be approved immediately,' are in truth approved because of their connexion with the disinterested affection of benevolence. Occasionally, it is true, he slips into such expressions as 'these [intransitive virtues] are immediately approved;' they 'are immediately recommended to our approbation by the constitution of our moral faculty' (p. 67) : but such incidental expressions, which are generally contradicted, implicitly or explicitly, in the same paragraph, only furnish evidence of the inadequacy of his analysis, and show that he himself had a dim impression

[1] *Lectures,* p. 65.

of the partial operation of the Moral Sense as expounded by him, and of its insufficiency to cover the whole nature of man.

Hutcheson next proceeds to show that the moral excellency of actions is, where 'equal degrees of happiness are expected to proceed from the action, in proportion to the *number* of persons to whom the Happiness shall extend ;' and is led to the conclusion that 'that action is best which accomplishes the greatest happiness for the greatest numbers, and that worst which in the like manner occasions their misery.' Again, where consequences are mixed, 'that action is good whose good effects preponderate over the evil.' By consequences we are to understand not only the direct effects of an action, 'but also all those events which otherwise would not have happened.' Hence we see that those actions are recommended to us by our Moral Sense as 'the most perfectly virtuous,' 'which appear to have the most universal unlimited tendency to the greatest and most extensive happiness of all the rational agents to whom our influence can extend.'

The exclusive contemplation of the instinct of benevolence as comprising all virtue, and as the sole object of the approbation of the Moral Sense, now begins to bear its fruit in Hutcheson's theory. The non-distinguishing of the virtuous sentiment of the moral agent from the object of his sentiment is also at work, and helps to bring into view the inadequacy of the original analysis from which the whole speculation started. For if the instinct of Benevolence is identical with Virtue, and if it be the object loved, and not the love of the object—the happiness effected, not the active sentiment of good-will, which is the object of approbation to the Moral Sense when it contemplates moral agents, it follows that the virtue of an act is a measurable quantity, and is measured by the quantity of happiness which flows from it. This consequence of his premisses Hutcheson accepts. The premisses themselves we have already criticised, and the consequences we might therefore pass by. But they suggest two remarks which find a fitting place here :—

First. We would observe that the moral purpose of the agent, and the act itself in its external incidence, are confounded. The claims of Morality and the demands of the Moral Sense are, it seems to us, satisfied, when the agent selects that motive which is the highest, and energizes under its direction. The *history* of the act is a separate question. A rational being is, of course, bound to see that the benevolent purpose has a benevolent effect, and his volition is not benevolent if he has no regard to this. Without this the moral energizing of the Will is an abortive energy. But it is the quality of this energizing which is the measure of the morality, not the number of persons who may be the happier or the better for it.

Some of the consequences of this quantitative conception of Virtue the author sees when he is driven to accept the greater quantity of good on the whole, as the only ground for abstaining from doing injustice to the worthless for the benefit of those who are morally their superiors, and from giving false testimony in a court of justice in favour of those whom we know to be innocent! A further consequence, namely, the inferior Virtue of the agent whose benevolent acts have a narrow influence, as compared with the man whose benevolent acts are productive of greater felicity, confronts him ; and he exercises much ingenuity in constructing mathematical canons for the assaying of personal virtue, by taking into account the various factors, Benevolence, the Moment of Good, and the Ability. It also follows, from his principles, that if a man, through a pure act of selfishness, or, it may be of hatred, purposes the misery of others, the Vice of that man is determined by the quantity of evil which he effects. Such results must always flow from a confounding of Agents and Acts, and from an insufficient Analysis of the inner moral history of man.

Secondly. We would remark that, according to Hutcheson, Virtue is Benevolence, and Benevolence Virtue. Benevolence is an Instinct, and Virtue, consequently, is also an Instinct. To what, then, is the Moral Sense reduced? To a feeling of higher pleasure in contemplating the Instinct of Benevolence than in contemplating other instincts. This separate faculty exists merely to tell us that Benevolence is better than Self-Interest. An admission of this nature New-Utilitarianism itself would scarcely hesitate to make. For the '*Social Sense*,' in which Mr. Mill finds the ultimate sanction and ground of Moral acts and of Virtue, is capable of being interpreted as Benevolence towards rational agents; and were we to accept this interpretation, the departure from Hutcheson's doctrine as Intuitional would be inappreciable. On every other point, in truth, save the question of an inner Sense (and even here the opposition is shadowy), we find the doctrine of Mr. Mill's *Treatise on Utilitarianism*, and of the most advanced views of Bentham in Hutcheson's *Inquiry*, developed with more precision, and argued with more regard to possible objections. We are thus driven to ask the question,—In such a system, does a Moral Sense, strictly so called, find any place at all? It seems to be reduced to an instinctive pleasure in the exhibition of an instinct,—a pleasure of a more intense kind than the pleasure which the agent has in other instincts.[1] It is admitted to be no guide to a man, in each particular act of life, much less in complex actions, or in 'the natural tendency of acts to good or evil' consequences. It consequently fails to discriminate the Right, and to be a guide to virtuous conduct. The work of guidance is delegated to the understanding, which, having fixed the external standard,—the 'greatest happiness on the whole,'—discovers, by a process of observation and reasoning, those acts which best fit the standard. The sole

---

[1] *System of Moral Philosophy*, p. 62.

function of the so-called Moral Sense, in short, in so far as it is distinct from purely intellectual operations, is 'to determine us to approve benevolence when it appears in any action, and to hate the contrary.'[1]

All this departure from the line of discovery on which he first entered, and by pursuing which he would have carried forward Shaftesbury and developed a moral system richer, more adequate, more full of the humanities than that of his contemporary Butler, is caused by his dread of recognising the subjective pleasure of beneficence as a virtuous end and motive of action. 'Not the pleasure which accompanies beneficence,' but the 'love of others,' he maintains, is true Virtue; as if the pleasure of beneficence could exist (save as an object of knowledge) apart from loving others; as if the active love of others did not itself constitute the very notion of beneficence. It was reserved to Butler to make a great advance beyond Hutcheson, and this advance would have been secured had he done nothing else than point out that Self-Love and Benevolence were not to be opposed, but only to be distinguished. In truth, one is sometimes disposed to doubt whether Hutcheson ever attained to a true conception of what was meant by allowing supremacy to the benevolent affections on the ground of their contributing to our own highest enjoyment. The following passages from his last and most matured work, his *System of Moral Philosophy*, give indications of this:—

[1] *Inquiry*, sect. 4.

'Can that be deemed the sole ultimate determination, the sole ultimate end, which the mind, in the exercise of its noblest powers, can calmly resolve with inward approbation deliberately to counteract? Are there not instances of men who have voluntarily sacrificed their lives, without thinking of any other state of existence, for the sake of their friends or their country? Does not every heart approve this temper and conduct, and admire it the more, the less presumption there is of the love of glory and posthumous fame, or of any sublimer private interest mixing itself with the generous affection? Does not the admiration rise higher the more deliberately such resolutions are formed and executed? All this is unquestionably true, and yet would be absurd and impossible if self-interest of *any kind* is the sole ultimate termination of all calm desire. There is therefore another ultimate determination which our souls are capable of, destined to be also an original spring of the calmest and most deliberate purposes of action; a desire of communicating happiness, an ultimate good-will not referred to any private interest, and often operating without such reference.

'In those cases where some inconsistency appears between these two determinations, the moral faculty at once points out and recommends the glorious, the amiable part; not by suggesting prospects of future interest of a sublime sort by pleasures of self-approbation or of praise. It recommends the generous part by an immediate, undefinable perception; it approves the kind ardour of the heart in the sacrificing even life itself, and that even in those who have no hopes of surviving, or no attention to future life in another world. And thus, where the moral sense is in its full vigour, it makes the generous determination to public happiness the supreme one in the soul with that commanding power which it is naturally destined to exercise.'

In these sentences Hutcheson seems to confound those collateral felicities and motives which accompany the benevolent affections with the felicity of benevolent affections and activity in themselves.

It is not necessary to our present purpose to follow the arguments by which Hutcheson endeavours to prove that Benevolence universally receives approbation, and the want of it reprobation ; and that seeming exceptions are to be traced to the mere semblance of Benevolence having been mistaken for the reality. Every moral theory has to accept the fact of moral growth and of diversity of moral practices, and to account for them ; a superfluous labour, it seems to us, except in so far as it throws light on the history of ethical science. For it is at once evident that whatever moral forces man may bring with him into the world, the material in which he works is so various and so manifold that the moral issue in maxims of conduct for the individual and the State must take the colour of circumstances, and accept the limitations of experience. We pass on to the next subject of speculative interest, our author's theory of Obligation.

In this region of moral inquiry, we again gladly find ourselves in the company of the vindicator of a Moral Sense as innate in Man. The departure from this doctrine and its consequences, which pervades two-thirds of his *Inquiry*, and which is, to our thinking, quite inconsistent with his leading position, here ceases, and in his concluding chapter, on the Obligation to Virtue, if not satisfactory, he is at least original and in harmony with himself. If there be, he says, an instinctive determination to approve virtuous (benevolent) action, and a determination to be uneasy with ourselves if we perform the contrary of it, this constitutes an Obligation. It does not take the form of a *Law* proceeding from a superior, and accompanied by sanctions; but it is none the less an Obligation implanted in us. And, even should we be of opinion that obligation can be properly said to exist only where there is a motive touching our *Self-interest* so closely as to determine us to a specific course of action, the obligation is then to be found in *reflection* on the pleasure which Virtue (benevolence) yields, and the uneasiness and dissatisfaction which accompanies and follows action contrary to virtue. A further motive of self-interest may be found in a consideration of the manner in which the good of the whole affects each individual, and consequently ourselves. We have preferred to use our own words in setting forth Hutcheson's view of the obligation to virtue, because, by so doing, we are able to bring more into relief its bearing on our previous exposition. If mental weakness, or ignorance, or selfish passions overpower the instinctive tendency to virtue, the business of the moral philosopher, says our author, is to enlighten the understanding, and to show that it is our true self-interest and advantage to be virtuous; not that the philosopher thereby hopes to stir to virtue, which is beyond his power, and because virtue followed from a perception of its advantage would be no longer virtue, but merely to remove the obstacles which obstruct the free movement of the innate tendency. Law, and laws with their external sanctions, may, in such cases, be necessary for the support of virtue. That law or laws, however, do not constitute any course of action good and right, is evident from the fact that we are constantly inquiring into the justice of laws, human and divine; and speak of the laws of God as just, and holy, and good, not because they are His will, but because they tend to the good of man.[1]

Thus, Hutcheson's answer to the question, 'Why should a man act virtuously (benevolently)?' is, 'Because he is so constituted that he has the pleasure of self-approbation if he so acts, and the displeasure of self-reprobation if he does not so act.' Other collateral and external obligatory forces may and do exist, are

---

[1] Hutcheson makes a distinction between constraint and obligation, in which he is not quite successful; and proceeds to apply his doctrine of Virtue (benevolence) to Perfect and Imperfect Obligations, making use of the correlative terms and notions, Perfect and Imperfect Rights.

brought into operation in every community, and are probably never quite lost sight of by any individual; but the inner, central, and primary obligation is that given above. But suppose a man should *prefer* that aggregate of happiness which unmixed self-interest can secure for him, and put up with the (to him) trifling pain of offended Benevolence, what is to be done? We then bring in, Hutcheson would say, the *external* sanctions of society, and the ultimate sanction of Divine approval and condemnation,—the law of Virtue being the law of God,—and the refractory agent submits, under the influence of these external forces, to yield an external conformity. But, in such a case, he has manifestly not yielded to the obligation of virtue *in itself*: he has recognised no supreme authority in it: he is hedged in to virtuous action by considerations human and divine, which lie outside virtue. In short, Hutcheson does not analyse the notion of Moral *Law*, and hence a conspicuous defect in his theory of obligation.

His analysis of 'Merit,' to which he next calls our attention, is vitiated by his conception of Virtue as something identical with Virtuous Sentiment, and, above all, with one particular Virtuous Sentiment, and by the further association of the notion of merit with a deserved recompense proceeding from God.

In casting a retrospect over the preceding pages, we must at once admit that Hutcheson occupies a distinguished place in the history of Ethical Science.

A certain portion of the ground traversed by him has been thoroughly occupied, and forms a starting-point for other thinkers. He has proved that there is in man a Moral Sense, in the signification of a Feeling of *immediate* pleasure on the perception of certain acts and affections, and a Feeling of *immediate* displeasure on the perception of their contraries. He has proved also that this sense is uniform to this extent—that benevolence is a quality *universally* approved in ourselves and others. And, further, he has shown that this benevolence is an instinct of man, having for its immediate object the happiness of others as an ultimate end, just as self-love has for object our own happiness. Nor has he rendered slight service to Morals by endeavouring to construct a theory of obligation on the basis of the inner affection or instinct apart from external sanctions and arbitrary law of whatsoever kind. Unfortunately his native subtlety of mind, concurring with a disposition of peculiar amiability, caused him, it seems to us, to overreach himself, and to fall into errors, several of which we have already noticed, and which again, in their more general aspects, fall to be pointed out in entering on a criticism of his contemporary, Bishop Butler.[1]

[1] Not the least of Hutcheson's services to morals is his subtle and successful criticism of Clarke and Woolaston.

THE ETHICAL THEORY OF BISHOP BUTLER.[1]

The current of philosophical thought in the end of the seventeenth and the beginning of the eighteenth century set in the direction of the inquiry, 'What constitutes Morality or Virtue?'—in other words, 'What is that common quality in acts which makes them Moral or Virtuous?' To combat, by superseding, the selfish and Utilitarian theories of morals, was the purpose of both Hutcheson and Butler, and of many other writers. The cognate question, 'By what inner process of Intelligence or Feeling do we cognize the virtuous act?' was to a large extent involved in the inquiry into Virtue. Hutcheson satisfied himself by finding an external standard of the virtuous act, which was free, as he rejoiced to think, from all taint of Self, and distinguished by the fact that other rational agents than Self furnished the motives to Virtue. In trying to work out his theory, he made such violent efforts to escape selfism, that he fell by anticipation into a kind of refined Benthamism, barely recovering himself when he came to the question of the Obligation to perform the virtuous act.

[1] To what extent Butler was indebted to Hutcheson does not appear. The Moral treatise of the former appeared in 1725, and in 1726 appeared the first edition of Butler's *Sermons*, which, however, had been preached some years before. In the preface to his second work, *On the Nature and Conduct of the Passions*, Hutcheson says,—'I hope it is a good omen of something still better on this subject to be expected in the learned world, that Mr. Butler, in his Sermons in the Rolls Chapel, has done so much justice to the wise and good order of our Nature.'

This was not the sole defect of his theory: the 'Moral Sense,' or Conscience, as exhibited in his argument, falls short of its proper function as a discerner of good and evil, except in the one department of benevolent activity. The system fails also to furnish a sufficient primary obligation to the virtuous act, and reduces duty to a question of secondary and external sanctions. It fails, further, in its definition of Virtue, and, like Shaftesbury's, is too narrow in its conception of the ends of human action. These defects are to be traced to the author's abhorrence of any form of subjective ethics, by which the motives and obligations of human conduct might by any possibility be referred to the pleasure which the agent has in Virtue. Had he taken a more impartial view of man's nature, —perhaps had he been a less amiable and virtuous man himself,—he might have seen that reference to self is not necessarily selfism; that self-interest and self-love are by no means identical terms; and that action in accordance with the latter demands all the self-abnegation which even a Stoic would require.

It was Butler's merit to endeavour to make good these defects, as well as those other shortcomings which we have pointed out in Shaftesbury; to seize in one comprehensive grasp the whole emotional and intellectual nature of man in its reference to the moral condition of the subject-self; to affirm a primary source of obligation in the form of a dictum of the Moral Sense or Conscience, and in the same Conscience a power of discerning right from wrong, not merely in actions benevolent, but in every kind of action, whether having its ultimate issue in the agent himself or in those outside him. He escaped Selfism on the one side, and objective Utilitarianism on the other, by placing the source and the authority of the Right in the arbitrary dicta of Conscience, and by showing that the highest end of action was conformity to Duty, on which happiness was only an attendant.

Such are the general characteristics of Butler's theory; and yet, if we are not to remain content with what appears on the surface and is conspicuous to the most cursory reader, but demand things instead of words, reasoned conclusions instead of asseverations, we shall find it by no means an easy task to give a clear, adequate, well-balanced statement of the author's system. He is very far from making a consistent use of terms, nor does he always introduce the various points of his argument in the connexion in which we should expect to find them. These and other defects, which belong to him as a writer on Morals, are, doubtless, to a large extent due to the form into which he has thrown his speculations. Had he attempted a more systematic exposition he would have supplied many defects which the mere attempt to systematize would have revealed. It is a remarkable tribute to his strong intellectual grasp and deep insight, that views so imperfectly expounded should have held their place as on the whole the best British statement of the intuitive theory of Morals.

Butler considers it to be the first duty of the Moralist to inquire what the particular nature of man is—its 'several parts,' and their economy or constitution,—and thence to determine what course of life it is which is correspondent to his *whole* nature. Such an inquiry, he maintains, will reveal the fact that Vice is a violation of that nature, and that Virtue consists in following it.

The economy or constitution of any particular nature, and consequently of the nature of man, is a whole made up of several parts; but these several parts taken together do not give the idea of the system or economy, unless we include in the notion of the whole the *relations and respects* which the several parts have to each other.

The several parts of the inward economy of man are Appetites, Passions, Affections, and, *in addition to these*, the 'Principle of Reflection,' or Conscience. But these several parts do not give us an idea of the inward economy of man until we realize their relations to each other. In investigating this we find that all the parts are subordinated to the 'Principle of Reflection' or Conscience, which is supreme. Thus we attain to a *complete* idea of the economy of man: and 'from the idea itself it will as fully appear that the end of the economy of man is Virtue, as that the end of the economy of a watch is the measuring of time. So that we shall find that nothing is so contrary to man's nature as vice, and nothing more accordant with it than virtue,' provided we keep in mind that by 'nature' we mean not merely the several parts of man's 'frame,' but the constitution of those parts relatively to the 'Principle of Reflection,' or Conscience.

Comparing man with the brutes, Butler illustrates his own theory and repeats his argument, and if we would estimate these correctly, we must once more accompany him in his exposition :—Mankind, he says, have various instincts and 'principles of action,' just as brute creatures have, some leading most directly and immediately to the good of the community, and some most directly to private good. Man has several, which brutes have not, particularly Reflection or Conscience —'an approbation of some principles or actions, and a disapprobation of others.' 'Brutes obey their instincts or principles of action according to certain rules, suppose the constitution of their body and the objects around them. The generality of mankind also obey their instincts and principles of action, all of them— those propensions we call good, as well as the bad— according to the same rules, namely the constitution of their body and the external circumstances they are in.' Now brutes, in acting in accordance with the rules before mentioned—their bodily constitution and circumstances—act suitably to their *whole* nature. Mankind also, in acting thus, would act suitably to their *whole* nature if no more were to be said of man's nature than what has now been said ; if that, as it is a true, were also a complete and adequate account of his nature. But it is *not* a complete and adequate account.

In addition to these instincts and principles of action which promote the interests of self, but do *not* flow from 'Self-love,' and those which promote the interests of others, but do *not* flow from Benevolence, there are the principles of 'Self-love' and 'Benevolence;' the former self-regarding, the latter other-regarding. Further, man is so constituted that he cannot intelligently seek the objects of self-love without embracing Benevolence and the social affections. Now, to follow the suggestions of all these 'instincts' and 'principles' is, in a certain sense, natural; but when we consider that, as a matter of fact, to gratify 'cool and reasonable self-love' is manifestly to act in conformity with nature, while to gratify appetites and passions in opposition to the dictates of 'cool self-love' is manifestly to contravene nature, inasmuch as it ignores the *relations* of the parts of human nature, it follows that one inward principle, that of 'cool self-love' is superior to others, is of a 'superior *nature*' or *kind:* and, also, that this natural superiority really exists quite apart from the degree of *strength* of the various principles, and this without particular consideration of conscience.

But this is not all. For there is still this other Principle in the human constitution,—namely, Reflection or Conscience,—which, compared with the rest as they all stand together in the nature of man, 'plainly bears on it' marks of authority over all the rest, and claims the 'absolute direction of them all to allow or forbid their gratification.' *Authority,* says Butler, as distinguished from strength; for a disapprobation of Reflection is in itself a principle *manifestly* superior to a mere propension—that is to say, superior in *kind* or *nature*, not in degree of force. If this be so, it follows that to allow no more to this superior principle or 'part of our nature' than to other parts, to let it guide and govern only occasionally, and in common with the rest as its turn happens to come, and from the temper and circumstances one happens to be in,—this is not to act conformably to the constitution of man.

The 'Principle of Reflection' or Conscience asserts, in the presence of consciousness, a natural supremacy over all other instincts and principles; and to this natural supremacy and inherent prerogative, 'it is owing that every man may find within him the rule of Right,' as well as the 'obligation to follow it.' This principle of reflection is frequently, but without deliberate purpose, spoken of by Butler as the principle of *Reflex Approbation*, when he has occasion to refer to the discrimination of the Right from the Wrong. In speaking of Shaftesbury, for example, he says that that author thought it a plain matter of fact 'that mankind upon reflection felt an approbation of what was good and a disapprobation of the contrary; as it undoubtedly is, and which none could deny but from mere affectation.' So much for Butler's doctrine of the ends of action, the criterion of Right and the mode of discriminating it.

The *Obligation* to do that which is approved is

inherent in the Reflex Act according to our author: and we have only to take into account '*the authority and obligation which is a constituent part of the* Reflex Approbation, and it will undeniably follow, though a man should doubt of everything else, yet that he would still remain under the nearest and most certain obligation to the practice of virtue: an obligation implied in the very idea of virtue, in the very idea of Reflex Approbation.' Certain propensions, selfish or other-regarding, may be as strong as the Principle of Reflection, but the latter is, by its very nature, manifestly superior to them, ' insomuch that you cannot form a notion of this faculty, Conscience, without taking in judgment, direction, and superintendency.' ' To preside and govern, from the very economy and constitution of man, belongs to it. Had it strength as it has right; had it power as it has manifest authority, it would absolutely govern the world.'

On the question of Conscience as a distinct faculty, there can be no doubt that Bishop Butler held the popular doctrine. With him the Principle of Reflection is to be confounded neither with self-consciousness nor with feeling in any form. At the same time, he admits that it shares some of its characteristics with ordinary reflection, for in an attempt which he makes to define it, he distinguishes it as 'a particular kind of reflection,' and in the Dissertation on Virtue he speaks of it as including the 'understanding' and the 'heart.'

If ethical questions, which are in their nature distinct, are in the above analysis occasionally allowed to cross each other, the reader may be assured that it is impossible altogether to avoid this confusion, if Butler's theory is to be given as conceived by himself. It would be possible, doubtless, so to evolve his doctrine as to give it a quasi-scientific form, and thereby a greater consistency of expression; but any attempt in this direction would expose us to the danger of losing sight of our author altogether, and inadvertently substituting interpretations of his theory for the theory itself.

In the exposition which we have given there have come into sufficient prominence those characteristics of Butler's argument which have obtained for it so wide a reception. We shall, accordingly, confine our criticism to the exhibition of its defects; and we shall best show what these are by directing attention to the answers which it affords to some of the leading moral questions.

The first and most conspicuous defect in the argument, is the adoption by Butler of what is neither more nor less than the 'vulgar' Conscience in its complex form under the name of the 'Principle of Reflection.' No attempt is made to analyse either this notion or, incidentally, any of the elements which enter into it. The same remarks apply to the highest object which the Conscience can contemplate—virtue. Hence not a little vicious circular reasoning and much perplexity to any reader who insists on a precise use of terms. At one time the Principle of Reflection appears as a simple principle, power, or instinct, undefined and unlimited; at another it does duty as the Feeling of approbation and disapprobation; again as the discriminator of right from wrong; at another as the authoritative or law-giving sentiment, while occasionally it is represented as discharging functions which belong rather to the understanding. This defective analysis, however, of the central subject and object of discussion is not a special characteristic of Butler, but is shared with him by a large proportion both of intuitional and utilitarian Moralists. Whenever it is met with, it must always be impossible to find a true record or accurate exposition of the phenomena of ethical consciousness.

The position in the moral economy which Butler assigns to Self-love next attracts our attention. The distinction between Selfishness and Self-love solves, for him, the question of interested and disinterested action by justifying his statement, that interestedness and disinterestedness are not properly to be opposed, but only to be distinguished. Self-love embraces a due consideration of our *whole* nature, including the benevolent and other sentiments; and as it thus necessarily includes the good of others, it is incorrectly confounded with Selfishness. So far as it goes, the distinction made by Butler is valuable; but it has the defect of not adequately explaining, either to the common consciousness or the scientific, the real ground on which any particular act is called 'disinterested,' although by its implicit assumption of the duality of human feeling it points the way to the explanation.

Still less success has attended our author in separating acts in respect of their quantitative or qualitative elements: a defect in his argument, which from the first precludes a consistent distinguishing of those manifestations of Self-Love which are, properly speaking, *prudential* from those which are in a special sense moral.

The most fertile source of confusion, however, is to be found in the position assigned to Self-love as a regulative principle. 'Cool self-love,' it would appear, determines the act which is to be preferred: in other words, it is competent to determine *duty:* but if it does this on grounds of Self-love, it follows that the sovereign end of man is happiness, virtue being comprehended as an end only *in so far as it is* the supreme happiness. Not only so: in the act of determining duty it must *ipso facto* exercise a governing power over the Principle of Reflection itself. This great Principle, accordingly, while it may still retain its place in the human economy, as what may be called an instinct of Reflection, can demand consideration from 'cool Self-love' only as one of many claimants. Doubtless its right to be distinguished from the 'propensions' as of a 'superior nature' to them would remain; and this characteristic would have to be taken into account by Self-love. But, even allowing for this, it seems clear that Conscience and Virtue would fall under the higher genus Self-love, which would control these 'principles' no less than all others. If, on the other hand, 'cool Self-love' be not supreme, the 'Principle of Reflection' supersedes its action entirely, not only in its larger acceptation, but even if interpreted as equivalent only to Prudence. For this principle being *all*-discriminating, and indicating instantaneously and with unerring finger not only generic qualities of acts, but the rightness of each particular act, Self-love becomes superfluous in the economy of man, and its pretensions irrelevant and impertinent. And yet so far is this limited and subordinate action of Self-love from being Butler's understanding of its function, that a careful perusal of different parts of his sermons will satisfy the reader that he regards it as not only embracing within its legitimate sphere of action the sentiments, but as being (1.) reflective, (2.) perceptive of ends, and (3.) capable of giving to various ends that *proportionate* importance on which throughout his writings he so frequently insists. If such be its function, it is consequently entitled to take cognisance of the Principle of Reflection, Approbation, or Conscience itself (all these are, with Butler, identical terms) and to assign it its true place and its proper influence. It thus becomes a conscience above a conscience.

The Principle of Reflection, Butler would doubtless say, if pressed by hostile criticism, designates that which is Duty and Virtue, without regard to Happiness ; while Self-love, on the other hand, has Happiness alone in contemplation. Happiness is a *consequence* of the full recognition of the law of duty, and thus it is that the Principle of Reflection and the

Principle of Self-love coincide. Although it is not specifically stated, it yet flows from the nature of the Principle of Reflection and the functions assigned to it, that the happiness of duty-doing is not considered to be the motive-power which ought to influence a moral agent, if indeed the happiness can be said to enter into the moral sphere at all in the strict and stoical sense. The contradiction, however, is not yet reconciled.

Notwithstanding the inconsistencies and inadequacies of statement which we have pointed out, there can be no doubt that in Butler's mind 'The Principle of Reflection' was the supreme moral faculty, the director and superintendent of all human action, always present and always asserting its presence. It is impossible to say, however, what ultimate definition Butler would have given of this principle, or how he would have characterized it, in the presence of adverse criticism. Probably he would have pointed to its characterization of itself in daily and hourly action within the breast of every man. That it is a 'particular kind of reflection,' seems to be admitted; and from this we may infer that its mode of procedure is a *process*, not an act. The first step is deliberation; that is, the holding before the mental view two or more differing, if not contradictory, acts, with a view to the discovery of that act which, being right, it behoves us to perform. Thus far we have to deal with an act of ordinary intelligence, the distinctive features of which appear only in the next step of the process, which is an instantaneous discrimination of the right, the moment it is compared with other possible courses of conduct. As the first step is simply a special application of the understanding, it follows that we begin to learn what this special faculty or 'Principle' is only in the second step, when it is manifestly a movement of Feeling. That by which we discriminate, then, must be a Moral Feeling or Sense.

How does this Feeling discriminate? According to Butler, by approving one thing and disapproving another. This appears from his own explicit statements, as well as from the fact that he constantly designates the 'Principle of Reflection' as the Principle of 'Reflex-Approbation.' Now, to discriminate by approving is to discriminate by an affection of feeling which is pleasurable; from which it follows that subjective happiness is, after all, the end of conduct, and the criterion of morality. If we bear in mind the range and function which Butler claims for Self-Love, it will be apparent that he cannot escape from the above interpretation of his position.

He himself would probably, however, resile from the conclusion to which we have brought him, and take refuge in the *Authority* of Conscience or the Principle of Reflection. The thing which is discriminated is, he might say, the *Authoritative* character of one act as compared with others ;—this feeling of Authority being in itself neither pleasurable nor painful, but simply a new thing, a new inner sensation, to which the name *Authority* is attached. But in the course of his argument to show that the Principle of Reflection holds supremacy over man's nature, he illustrates it by the principle of Self-Love, which also has, according to him, a claim to supremacy, by virtue of the fact that the pleasure it yields is of a superior *kind* to that of the 'propensions,' etc. In this superiority of *kind* lies its superiority of rightful power; in other words, its inner authority. From this we are led to perceive that the supremacy of Conscience is determined by its superiority in nature and kind to other principles of action, and that on this superiority rests its claim to supreme authority. But, setting aside the element of intellect in this 'Principle of Reflection,' I am at a loss to know how I can become aware of its superiority of *kind* as one of many feelings, save by a finer *quality* of sensation being yielded by it. Thus, whatever may be said of duty and authority, the Principle of Reflection, so far as it discriminates or discerns, finally resolves itself into understanding *plus* a feeling of pleasure or pain; and thus we are again brought round to the conclusion that happiness is the criterion of rightness.

Having found our criterion and our discerning *Feeling*, we have the means of discriminating the Right in each particular case. But having found them, we next ask, 'Why should a man conform to the right?' In the preceding exposition we have found Butler's answer to this question to be, that 'Conscience not only shows us the way, but carries its authority with it, or, we might rather say, *in* it.' Here the chief defect of Butler is the acceptance of such an inner sentiment without any attempt to analyse it, or to trace out its various manifestations with a view to ascertain its real character. Whether this authority *proceeds from* the fact of the superiority in *kind* of that principle of action which has been already discerned in the second step of the conscience-process to be the right principle, and therefore may be resolved into the obligation or authority which is inherent in admitted *ends* as such (an authority which Butler elsewhere maintains), or arises in consciousness close in the rear of the discernment of the right, or concurrently with it; or whether, in fine, it leaps out of the heart of the perception of rightness as *part of the act* of moral perception, saying in a voice of thunder, 'Do this,'— does not appear. We are merely told that it is 'a constituent part of Reflex-approbation.' We are consequently at a loss to know how to argue the question with our author, unless we were to take up for criticism the current intuitive doctrine of 'Conscience-authority,' and identify his opinion with it,—a course of procedure which would scarcely be justifiable. We must therefore content ourselves with the above exposition of Butler's special errors of confusion on this the most important of ethical questions. Where we expected to find strength we have found weakness— strength of asseveration doubtless, but a slurring over of difficulties and an inadequate psychological analysis.

Nor do we obtain more satisfaction when we question our author on the 'Supreme Good.' The Supreme Good vanishes into conformity with the dictates of 'cool Self-love *and* Conscience,' and its unity is thus broken, while virtue is identified (as is too common in ethical writings), with virtuous sentiments at one time, virtuous conduct or conduct in harmony with nature in the stoical sense at another, and with conscience itself at a third. So far is this negligence carried, that we find such loose expressions as the following:—Obligation is 'implied in the very idea of Virtue, in the very idea of Reflex-approbation.' In what sense obligation is contained in the idea of Virtue apart from Reflex-approbation or Conscience is not explained, and we are thus compelled to identify conscience and the object of its contemplation, virtue.

In truth we find, the more closely we look into Butler's theory, that there is in it a threefold system of parallel and concurrent ends and obligations. Our criticism on the position in the human economy which he assigns to Self-Love, as a regulative and authoritative principle, justifies this conclusion when taken in connexion with his theory of Virtue. For he informs us that man's nature is 'plainly adapted' to virtue, and that we are bound to harmonize our actions with nature if we would fulfil the *end* of our economy,—the obligation to the pursuit of this end lying in the admitted fact that it *is* an end. And alongside of both these moral theories we have an overriding and dominant system, of which the leading characteristic is a separate Faculty or Principle of Reflection, at once discriminating, authoritative, and the supreme end in itself.

Passing from the questions of ends, of criterion, and of obligation to the question of Conscience, as a separate faculty, we find that little need be said. In our author this vague and indefinite original power is, if we look closely, found to be composed of four elements, undistinguished the one from the other, and to be by no means that simple ultimate power which his followers usually assume, supported in this assumption by their master's example. It reflects, it discriminates, it approves, it commands. Which of these functions truly exhibits to our view the separate moral faculty?

In concluding this brief critical survey of Butler's argument, we are struck by the fact that he owed more to Shaftesbury and Aristotle than to any other philosopher. To Shaftesbury he owes, among other things, the idea of an inner constitution and harmonious end, while a reminiscence of Aristotle runs through his whole conceptions. His 'principles of action' are, generally speaking, the non-rational impulses and affections of Aristotle; and where Aristotle placed controlling reason actively seeking a mean in all passions of the soul, Butler placed the Principle of Reflection—an internal sense discharging the function of reason and also of a conscience. Even this position, however, he does not steadily and consistently adhere to; and the consequence is, that, after the most careful study, we close his book with the feeling that a powerful thinker has taken a firm grasp of moral truths, but that by contenting himself with the complex where he should have sought the simple, and by assuming where it was necessary to prove, he has failed to give forth a system which can stand the test of a close analysis.

TRANSITION TO BENTHAM.

DAVID HUME (died 1776).

Were we writing a history of moral speculation, we should here have to trace the influence of Locke, Leibnitz, and Wolf on the ethical thought of Europe. Our purpose, however, is much more limited. Having traced the rapid development of the Intuitional theory in reaction against the extreme sensationalism and cynical utilitarianism of Hobbes, we now propose to turn our attention to the revival of his doctrines in a new and much modified form by Bentham, and his successors in our own day, Mr. Mill and Mr. Bain. Intuitionalism continued to be well represented and ably taught by Adam Smith, Reid, Stewart, Brown (under certain reservations), and others; while Hartley, Tucker, and Paley stood forth as the most prominent exponents of the opposite school. The most interesting of the brilliant thinkers who crowded the latter half of the eighteenth century was David Hume. While giving the weight of his influence to utilitarianism, he more than any other illustrates the inroad which the writers whose labours we have reviewed had made on the Hobbistic doctrine. An anti-Hobbist he certainly is, and yet we are so far from classing him with Intuitionalists, that we find in him the philosophic groundwork of Benthamism. Although we do not propose to give a full exposition of his theory, a few words will help to indicate the historical connexion in this country between the eighteenth and the nineteenth century.

Notwithstanding the lucidity of David Hume's style, it is not always at once obvious how far his argument is intended to carry his readers, or what are the distinctive features of his theory. This arises, perhaps, from the attitude of analytic inquirer rather than of synthetic system-builder which he assumes. In ethics, this peculiarity of Hume's reasoning is, as might be expected from the complex nature of the subject, especially conspicuous. The following may be accepted as an accurate though brief statement of the conclusions to which he came, it being understood that his mode of expression is translated into more modern phraseology.

1. The Criterion of Morality Hume finds to be, so far as transitive or social acts are concerned, Utility; Utility, however, being only a means towards an end, and that end being the happiness and interests of society. The happiness and interests of society, accordingly, are the end and criterion of the Right in all social acts. Similarly, those acts which are not social have for their end and criterion the happiness and interests of the individual.

2. The foundation of what may be distinctively called 'Morality' of acts, viz., their approvableness, or the reverse, is, (*a.*) in the case of acts *social*, the

Sentiment of Humanity or Benevolence, which is the source of the pleasure we feel when acts are seen to attain the useful end. Sometimes it is merely the agreeable feeling which we have on seeing them in operation. But here Hume is manifestly loose in his analysis; for all cases of the 'agreeable' in the matter of transitive acts are resolvable into the satisfaction of the sentiment of Humanity. For example, the qualities of Decency, Cleanliness, Manner, Manners, Wit, which are referred to by Hume, are all of manifest objective utility. (*b.*) In the case of acts not social, the foundation of approvableness is the agreeableness of them to the person who performs them, and, consequently, to others who behold them in him. This presumes, of course, the doctrine of sympathy as essential to moral judgments, but he does not give the doctrine any prominence, or appear to see its full importance, except in one passage, where he says,—The 'immediate sensation [of the social qualities] to the person possessed of them is agreeable: others enter into the same humour, and catch the sentiment by a contagion or natural sympathy; and as we cannot forbear loving whatever pleases, a kindly emotion arises towards the person who communicates so much satisfaction.'[1] Those people are 'virtuous' and 'meritorious' who practise qualities which thus stir up in us agreeable feelings when we contemplate them and their operation. [The principal intransitive qualities cited as meritorious are

---

[1] Sect. vii. 'Of Qualities immediately agreeable to ourselves.'

Tranquillity, Greatness of Mind, Courage, Delicacy of Taste.]

3. The ground of *Obligation* to do the act which contributes to the end—the happiness of society or the interests and happiness of the individual agent, as the case may be—is this, that all men, if they will only see it, will 'find their account' in so acting. The virtuous is a pleasant, attractive, and much-rewarding mental condition; and it seems very absurd not to maintain oneself constantly in it. If men decline to do so, they will suffer from the disapprobation of their fellow-men, and from want of peace in themselves.

4. Reason instructs in the tendency of acts, and its operation is especially needful in all questions of Justice. When these are reduced to their simple elements, their relation to the happiness of society will be seen, and the Sentiment of Humanity will then affix to them the character of approvable or disapprovable. He maintains that presumed Justice only *may be*, whereas Benevolence must be always, useful to society; and that it is therefore difficult to say when an act is to be approved as Just.

Hume's position may be thus briefly summed up :—
'Morality is determined by Sentiment;' and 'Virtue' is 'whatever mental action or quality gives to a spectator the pleasing sentiment of approbation.' The next question in morals is, 'What actions have this influence on the spectator's sentiment?' And the answer is, 'Those which produce happiness and pro-

mote the interests of society.' The third question—the question of a moral faculty—is answered dubiously thus: 'The final sentence' as to the 'amiable or odious probably depends on some internal sense or feeling.'

Were we to endeavour to characterize Hume's ethics in their relation to his predecessors, we should say that it was an eclectic Epicureanism, modified by the 'Moral-Sense' doctrines of Hutcheson. Bentham specially repudiated all of Hume which seemed to point to the theory of a Moral Faculty, but he unquestionably owed to him the form of his own utilitarianism; while to the thoroughgoing system of Paley[1] he was indebted for the extension of the utilitarian ends and sanctions beyond the present existence.

---

[1] Died 1805. His doctrines are considered in the Notes on Professor Bain.

JEREMY BENTHAM.

BORN 1748; DIED 1832.

IN our opinion the distinctive characteristic of Jeremy Bentham's moral theory is the relation in which it stands to his systematic psychology. It is to the underlying scheme of the human mind, and to the implicit reference which is constantly made to it, that we owe the favourable contrast in which Benthamism stands to the theory of Hobbes. Had this contrast been more clearly seen, the merits of the author would have been more generously admitted by those whose opposition has been too often stimulated by party feeling.

Bentham held that Utility was the standard of the Right in conduct, personal and political. By the Utility of an act he meant its tendency to produce Happiness (pleasure, or rather the aggregate of pleasures) or to prevent Unhappiness (pain). This is nowhere more clearly and succinctly expressed than in the *Introduction to the Principles of Morals and Legislation*, where he says,—

'Nature has placed mankind under the government of two sovereign masters, pain and pleasure. It is for them alone to point out what we ought to do, as well as to determine what we shall do. On the one hand, the standard of right and wrong, on the other, the chain of causes and effects, are fastened to their throne. They govern us in all we do, in all we say, in all we think; every effort we can make to throw off our subjection will serve but to demonstrate and confirm it. In words a man may pretend to abjure their empire, but in reality he will remain subject to it all the while. The *principle of utility* recognises this subjection, and assumes it for the foundation of that system, the object of which is to rear the fabric of felicity by the hands of reason and of law.'

The degrading connotations which have gathered round the word Utility must be stripped off if we are to understand Bentham and his system, and the term must be employed in the sense which he attached to it. The same caution has to be given with reference to the word Interest. By the 'interest' of an individual or a community, Bentham meant the 'happiness' of an individual or community; nor did he restrict the application of the term 'happiness' to those lower pleasures which in vulgar acceptation are identified with 'utilities' and 'interests.'

In estimating Bentham's moral teaching, it is further necessary to bear in mind that, while of all thinkers it may be truly said that their character and the circumstances of their lives colour, if they do not determine, their thought, this may be said in a peculiar sense of those thinkers who begin and end with the practical, and who value their analysis only in so far as it is visibly fraught with beneficial consequences to society. Starting, as Bentham did, with a feeling of moral disgust at legal forms and fictions, stimulated on his career of speculation by a perception of the injustice which characterized, in his opinion, much of the administration of law, and by the departure, as it seemed to him, from all principle in the administration of affairs, unless a regard for the interests of the governing classes might be called such, his work of aggression would have been fragmentary, declamatory, and inconsistent with itself, had he not sought and found some distinctive and unvarying standard by which to test and harmonize his speculations,— some steady light to guide him through the perplexities of ethical and political discussion. That he was deeply sensible of this himself, and that to this we owe the purely ethical part of his writings, appears from the fact that the *Introduction to the Principles of Morals and Legislation* was originally printed under a different title and withheld from publication[1] partly in consequence of the metaphysical difficulties in which he found himself involved. Continuing, however, to pursue his legal and political studies, he found that in every one of his works the principles exhibited in the *Introduction* 'had been found so necessary, that either to transcribe them piecemeal or to exhibit them somewhere where they could be referred to in the lump was unavoidable.' Elsewhere he says, that there is not 'a single proposition that I have not found occasion to build upon in the penning of some article or other of those provisions of detail of

[1] Printed in 1780, published in 1789.

which a Body of Law, authoritative or unauthoritative must be composed.'

The ultimate standard of reference Bentham, as we have seen, found to be the pains and pleasures, the happiness and unhappiness of man. This was afterwards formulated into the 'Greatest Happiness of the Greatest Number,' and this again was at a later period improved into 'The Greatest Happiness on the Whole,'—a movement in Bentham's thought which seems to have escaped the notice of the majority of his disciples, but which was by no means without significance. He, however, never rested content, as the majority of his followers have done, with the vague phrase 'The Greatest Happiness of the Greatest Number.' On the contrary, he says that 'it is in vain to talk of the interest of the community without understanding what is the interest of the individual. A thing is said to promote the interest, or to be for the interest, of an individual when it tends to add to the sum-total of his pleasures, or, what comes to the same thing, to diminish the sum-total of his pains. An action, then, may be said to be conformable to the principle of utility, or, for shortness' sake, to Utility (meaning with respect to the community at large), where the tendency it has to augment the happiness of the community is greater than any it has to diminish it.'

Having thus rested the principle of Utility on the two pillars, pleasures and pains, and having affirmed the 'impossibility of understanding the interest of the Public Body without first understanding the interest of the individual bodies composing it,' he found it necessary, with a view to give completeness to his Ethical system, to inquire into the nature of the individual man.

In entering upon this analysis, he started from the point of view that morals and legislation had to do with psychological pathology alone, and that man must be regarded solely as a bundle of pleasures and pains, actual or possible. The results of his analysis he gives in a Table of the 'Springs of Action,' showing the several species of pleasures and pains of which man's nature is susceptible, together with the several species of interests, desires, and motives respectively corresponding to them. This table is followed by explanatory notes and observations, and must always be read in connexion with his statements of moral doctrine. It exhibits fourteen classes of Pleasures, with their corresponding pains, interests, and motives —a motive being a desire of securing some pleasure or interest, or of avoiding some pain. To enter into these in detail is not necessary to our present purpose. It will suffice, omitting what is meanwhile superfluous, to enumerate them. They are Pleasures and Pains of the Palate, with its corresponding interest of the palate; Pleasures and Pains of the sexual appetite, with its corresponding sexual interest; Pleasures and Pains of the Sense, generally or collectively considered, with the corresponding sensual interest; Pleasures and Pains of Possession and Privation, with the corresponding interest of the purse; Pleasures and Pains of

Power, with its corresponding interest of the sceptre; Pleasures and Pains of Curiosity, with its corresponding interest of the spying-glass; Pleasures and Pains of Amity, that is to say, derivable from the Good-will or Ill-will of others towards self, with the corresponding interest of the closet; Pleasures and Pains of the Moral or Popular Sanction (Reputation), with its corresponding interest of the trumpet; Pleasures and Pains of the Religious Sanction (that is to say, of religion, or the love and fear of God), with its corresponding interest of the altar; Pleasures and Pains of Sympathy (that is to say, of Benevolence or Good-will), with its corresponding interest of the heart; Pleasures and Pains of Antipathy (that is to say, of malevolence or ill-will), with its corresponding interest of the gall-bladder; Pains of Labour, with its corresponding interest of the pillow; Pains of Death, and bodily pains in general, with the corresponding interest of self-preservation; Pleasures and Pains of the self-regarding class, collectively considered, and the corresponding self-regarding Interest.

To show that this analysis is inadequate, that it exhibits too much as well as too little, that the cross-divisions are numerous, and that consequently, as a scheme of ethical psychology, it will not bear the slightest investigation, would be easy, were it within the scope of our present argument. The scheme, such as it is, however, merits our gratitude, and served Bentham's purpose. Having thus settled to his own satisfaction the various pleasurable and painful ends, and having defined a motive to be the desire of having or avoiding one or other of these ends, he thereby defined utility as a principle of conduct for the individual, and, by consequence, for states.

Pleasures, then, constituting the utilities, and Pains the inutilities, of human life, it behoves man to seek the former and avoid the latter, if he would do *right*. What! we feel constrained to ask, when reading such a simple summary of moral duty, Can it ever be right to court the pleasures of malevolence and antipathy, or to indulge, without stint, in the pleasures of the senses, or of power, or of the closet, or of the trumpet? Into the multitude of pleasures and pains of which man is susceptible, does no supreme controlling power enter? Sum up, says Bentham, the pleasures or utilities that flow from any act, and put them on one side of your moral ledger, and on the other make an equally careful summation of the pains or inutilities, strike the balance, and if it be on the side of Pleasure, it will give the *good* tendency of the act upon the whole, and thereby constitute it *right*; if on the side of Pain, it will give the *bad* tendency of it on the whole, and thereby constitute it *wrong*. Right and Wrong, Virtue and Vice, accordingly, become questions of measure and quantity. In perfect consistency with this doctrine, Bentham holds that there can be no such thing as good or bad motives, inasmuch, we suppose, as every possible motive which can actuate a man must be a desire for some admitted utility which is in itself good.

Now, so far as personal morality is concerned, that is to say, those states and acts which confine themselves to the individual alone, we are perfectly entitled to maintain that there can be, according to the above theory, neither good nor bad, approvable nor censurable, virtue nor vice, in any *moral* sense. A man may be careless or stupid, and cast up the columns of his conduct-ledger wrong; or he may be foolish, unwise, intellectually perverse: but nothing more and nothing worse.

This conclusion as regards Bentham's system of personal ethics is further justified by the purely external character of his moral Sanctions or Obligations; nor do we suppose it is one which any of his disciples would deny, except those who have acquired a habit of reading *into* Bentham what they have found elsewhere.

The cause of truth, however, is never advanced by straining the weak points of any system of thought, least of all ought there to be a disposition to do this in the case of an antagonist whose theoretical weaknesses arise from a too exclusive regard to the strengthening of his means of attack and defence on the side where his theory combated what seemed to him to be existing injustice, and promoted the cause of humanity. A more congenial task is to seek for indications, if any such can be found, of a truer and higher view of right and wrong in human conduct than can be extracted from the above summary.

Nor are such indications altogether wanting, although so introduced and so conceived as not substantially to affect the theoretical development of the author's doctrine of personal morality. Such indications may be found, for example, in his observations on 'Good and Bad,' etc., where he affirms each Pleasure to be a good in itself; that is, 'on the supposition that it is not *preventive* [not of a quantity of pleasure or pleasures, but] of a more than *equivalent pleasure;*' and again, in the *Principles of Morals and Legislation,* where, in reply to objections, he says, —'There are interests [pleasures or happinesses] of different orders, and different interests are in certain circumstances incompatible. Virtue is the sacrifice of a smaller to a greater interest.' The important ethico-psychological truths to which such passages point, although unrecognised in a systematic way by Bentham, manifestly influenced his thought; and, to an extent greater than he imagined, formed the basis of his own moral judgments, supplying unconsciously the defects of his system. When penning these qualifications of his theory, he, in point of fact, stood on the border-ground which separates the Benthamite system of objective utilitarianism from the higher doctrine of subjective eudæmonism; nay, he had almost obtained a glimpse of a system of eudæmonism which restored to man a Moral Sense, while finding in its larger interpretation of ethical consciousness a fitting place for quantitative or utilitarian ethics. Unfortunately, such glimpses as he seems occasionally to have obtained of the moral nature of the individual man, and of the true characteristics of the moral and virtuous act, were quickly lost sight of. Nor could anything else have been expected. That he should quickly pass from the consideration of the 'interest of the individual,' to which we have referred above, and which would have confined him for a time within the sphere of subjective ethics, arose from the fact that the work he had to do was in the field of political morality. Accordingly, he hurried on to the consideration of man as a constituent member of a body politic, and of his duties to the community as a subject or as a ruler, contemplating self-referent duties only in so far as they immediately or mediately affected the community at large.

It is in pursuit of this object that, when surveying the various pleasures of which man was susceptible, and each of which he might *rightly* indulge in its turn, it was necessary to find some limiting or controlling principle by which each man, as *a member of society*, must regulate his conduct; and further, to find certain sanctions, that is to say, obligatory or binding pleasures and pains wherewith to ratify and enforce the recognition of the principle. If man's acts were not to be regulated by ever-varying caprice, if moral distinctions were not to cease, if society was not to be a chaos of conflicting motives and ends all equally right and good, some supreme and regulative pleasurable end had to be found to which all others should subordinate themselves. That supreme end, that regulative standard, was the principle of Utility *par excellence*, the *Utility of the Community as a whole* dominating over all minor utilities,—the general as opposed to the particular well-being. Or, it may be technically put thus : if any man desires to gratify the interests of the senses, the spying-glass, the sceptre, or the altar, he must consider to what extent such gratification would affect the general quantity of pleasure in the State, and abstain if the balance be unfavourable. Thus the *extra-regarding* pleasures constitute a kind of outside conscience, and restrain or stimulate the *self-regarding* pleasures according to the circumstances of each case.

The first consequence which follows from this position is, that inasmuch as the act of each individual is to be estimated according to the quantity of pleasure or pleasures which it produces or tends to produce, it must often happen that many will suffer pains from an act which the summation of the two sides of the moral-ledger shows to be productive of pleasure to a still larger number, that is, to be productive of a larger mass of pleasures, and to be *therefore* right. Hence the inevitable necessity early imposed on Bentham and his disciples, of explaining Utility by the phrase, 'The Greatest Happiness of the Greatest Number,' a formula which was afterwards interpreted to mean 'The Greatest Happiness on the whole.'

Having thus fixed the ultimate end of individual and corporate action, and found the Utility which controlled other Utilities and gave them their *moral* character, the next question which presented itself for answer was, 'Why should a man conform to this Greatest-Happiness end?' To the reply, that so to conform was itself a pleasure, being in fact the pleasure of Good-will, already included in the classification of springs of action, the rejoinder might fairly be, that the individual, having made his moral summation, found his happiness-account in another course of conduct; in short, in the gratification of the self-regarding pleasures. Nor, on utilitarian ground, is it possible to overthrow this position, except by showing the recalcitrant, that if he framed his conduct in accordance with the Greatest-Happiness standard, he would be thereby simply taking the surest, though certainly a circuitous, way of securing for himself the greatest possible amount of selfish *personal* pleasures and the greatest possible amount of freedom from selfish personal pains. Thus altruism would become a mediate egoism. And this is substantially what Bentham tries to show, either explicitly or by implication, *passim*. He does so explicitly, when he enumerates the pleasures and pains which go to support and hedge round the supremacy of the Greatest-Happiness standard. These are his moral sanctions, and are classified as physical, political, moral, and religious. We do not mean to say that Bentham ever fairly and fully faces the question, 'Why should a man conform to the Greatest-Happiness standard?' but as our object is to state succinctly the most consistent and favourable theory of Benthamite utilitarianism, and as the only sanctions or binding forces of pain and pleasure which Bentham mentions are those just enumerated, we presume that they would be used, in case of polemical need, as furnishing the best utilitarian answer to the question, 'Why is a man to do right?'

The sanctions above referred to are not specially introduced by Bentham as the binding forces naturally operating to cause men to conform to the Greatest-Happiness end, but they are exhibited and expounded as the sanctions of utilitarianism generally, and it accordingly follows that they are operative in obliging individuals to a submission of their wills to the fundamental or ultimate principle of all right human conduct. On this presumption, then, we turn to look at these sanctions more closely, and find that if a man does not do right, he may or will suffer— (1.) Physical pains; that is, such material calamities as befal a man in the order of nature, in consequence of his own imprudence: (2.) Political pains; that is, such pains as may be inflicted on him by a judge: (3.) Moral pains; that is, such pains as may visit him, because not warded off by the consideration which other people with whom he has intercourse have for his character: (4.) Religious pains; that is, such pains as may visit him here or hereafter, in consequence of the wrath of God. Now a careful consideration of the aims and tendency of Bentham's writings will satisfy any man that, in the above theory of obligation, he did not do justice to himself, still less to the utilitarian ethics. Any attempt, however, to extract out of the materials which he has furnished a more adequate and more acceptable theory of moral ends and obligations, would be to make him see what the persistency and pertinacity of the attitude which he took up (in consequence of his practical aims) prevented his seeing; it would be, in short, to present to the reader a natural development of Benthamism instead of Benthamism proper. We must note, therefore, that these sanctions of the Right are purely material and external—*penal* in the ordinary acceptation of this word. Were any of the numerous disciples, who have unconsciously imported something of themselves into their master's doctrine, to doubt this, the following extract from the *Principles of Morals and Legislation* would settle the doubt :—

'Of these four sanctions, the physical is altogether, we may observe, the groundwork of the political and moral: so is it also of the Religious, in as far as the latter bears relation to the present life. It is included in each of those other three. This may operate in any case (that is, any of the pains or pleasures belonging to it may operate) independently of *them;* none of *them* can operate but by means of this. In a word, the powers of nature may operate of themselves; but neither the magistrate, nor men at large, *can* operate; nor is God, in the case in question, *supposed* to operate, but through the powers of nature.' See also his *Logical Arrangements*.

It is scarcely necessary to add, that by the same means corresponding pleasures induce men to prefer the Right.

There can be no doubt that, so far as *personal morality* is concerned, Benthamism puts no check on the indulgence of the various pleasures and interests, beyond those which the idiosyncracies and circumstances and calculations of individuals might of themselves put, until the gratification of them is found to hurt the general utility. Further, that its governing principle has no *inherent* value or attraction, but derives its supremacy *from the general perception of common interests, and the pains which the general opinion inflicts on the purely self-regarding citizen;* that, consequently, the only obligation to do the Right is to be found in those external sanctions of pain and pleasure which are dependent on the action of *others*, and which affect for better or worse the numerous susceptibilities of the human constitution, as they have been already detailed by him in his pathological psychology. While these conclusions regarding the system are correct, if the system be judged from the works of the author, we must at the same time guard the reader against confounding this theory of Use with the theory of mere pleasure and pain in any Cyrenaic sense. Benthamism is not hedonism. It is a system of calculation of quantities, in which, it is true, all the quantitative elements are originally of the same value, but, unlike Hobbism, it embraces Good-will (Amity) and Love of Reputation, thereby connecting us sympathetically with our fellow-men.

The defects of the theory, as a theory of ends and obligations, we have to some extent indicated in the course of our exposition, and others it would be superfluous in these days to dwell upon. The cardinal objections to the system, quite apart from its utter inadequacy as an analysis of the moral nature of man,—a subject which might furnish a topic for many chapters of disquisition,—may be brought into view in a comparatively limited space.

As a theory of Ends, it is based on an inaccurate psychology, inasmuch as it does not allow the Qualitative to enter into the argument at all, much less as a supreme regulative element. The higher and lower disappear, and all morality is merged in prudence. This radical defect we have already noticed in the course of our exposition.

The system makes no distinction, except incidentally, between Subjective or Intransitive, and Objective or Transitive acts, and while fixing a criterion for the latter, leaves the former without protection. In acts of the former class, accordingly, a moral agent is justified in acting in accordance with his intellectual summation alone, should he choose to stand by it and to aver that the interests of sense are more to him than all others aggregated. Nay, even in acts Transitive, the criterion furnished is quite illusory, because the *kind* of happiness which an individual might choose to promote in the community, under a *bona fide* desire to comply with the criterion, may be based on inadequate, low, and erroneous conceptions. His desire to distribute happiness will not enable him to distribute anything better than his own conception of what is best, which conception rests, and must rest on his own experiences of felicity alone, and his own conclusions about it, which, as appears from what we have said as to subjective acts, *may* be low and erroneous. We cannot venture safely to enter on the question of the distribution of happiness until we have settled the question of individual happiness for ourselves; that is to say, until we have formed a conception of human life and destiny.

If the happiness to be distributed has not this foregone subjective basis, it must rest on the will of the community which we wish to benefit; but inasmuch as this means the opinion, for the time being, of the majority, and inasmuch as each member of the majority may have made an erroneous quantitative summation, and the minority may after all be right, it follows that there is no fixed basis for the right transitive act which can approve itself to any rational intelligence.

Even supposing that each man were gifted with supreme prudence, and could determine for himself that *quantitative aggregation* of pleasures which was greatest, therefore best, and therefore for himself, as man, the right and moral end, yet Good-will and sympathy, although they would, according to the Benthamite scheme, enter into this aggregation, could not *rightly* do so in any dominant or prevailing way. When, therefore, required to conform in his *transitive* acts to the greatest happiness of the greatest number, he would be morally justified in declining to do so, on the ground that it interfered with his happiness on the whole, until he was *convinced* that his own personal aggregate pleasures would be extended or intensified by so acting; in other words, that the twelve classes of interests, which have nothing to do with the interest of Amity or the love of Reputation, would gain by the transaction more than they lost.

If *he were not convinced*, and yet were compelled to obey laws which were based on the *common interests*, he might justly complain of injustice, and society itself would be guilty of immorality in his special case. If *he were convinced*, the right transitive acting of to-day might become wrong transitive acting to-morrow, and meanwhile the delicate quantitative balance be disturbed by a keener relish for some of the self-regarding interests of Sense, or of Power, or what not. The Prudence of to-day would be the Imprudence of to-morrow. Even should he remain in the same mind and conviction, the gratification of the benevolent and social interests, although yielding a certain limited reward *in themselves*, would continue to be practised with a view to the reversion of the twelve self-regarding interests—would be, in short, an indirect or mediate selfishness, under a delusive and imposing name.

Further, the *obligation* so to act would rest solely on the threats of his fellow-men. It could not rest in himself, because the whole question with him has been one of *desirableness* only, not of imperativeness. Imperativeness can have no possible place in the inner history of his deliberations. Nor could it rest in the will of God, because, in so far as the will of God is revealed in the *order* of His constitution, it is revealed on the side of that which yields the greatest quantity of desirable things on the whole. And to the argument that, inasmuch as he does possess the 'interests' of Amity and Reputation, he is *ipso facto* under obligation to the Creator who implanted these in his heart to gratify them, it would be a sufficient answer to say that these were given to him merely to *help* him to do those transitive acts which, in an indirect way, might bring about the largest quantity of pleasures on the whole, and to reconcile him to temporary sacrifices with a view to large returns.

Accordingly, even supposing him to be convinced, there being no natural superiority in any of the forces and corresponding interests within him, there would be no inner sense of obligation or authority at all possible. The feeling of obligation would grow up only as he gradually realized the forces outside him prepared to make him suffer in his 'interests' if he did not do certain things; that is to say, there would be only external sanctions, and an external source of obligation. Nor only so: these sanctions or obligations would be derivative, not primary, by which I mean that the disapprobation of men would not act as an obligatory force upon him, but only the *consequences* of that disapprobation as these might touch his interests. The force of disapprobation or evil reputation, in itself or in its primary character, would doubtless operate to some extent; but as it is only one of fourteen separate interests, its presence would scarcely be discernible. In so far as it was discernible and operative to the extent of more than one-fourteenth, it would indicate moral weakness in the individual who was so influenced, inasmuch as he allowed one or two quantitative elements to overbear so many others of equal importance. The model moral man would, in fact, display his virtue by giving this 'interest' a very inferior force, just as the same man would exhibit his virtue by giving twelve personal interests supremacy over 'Amity' and 'Reputation' in the case of transitive acts, except in so far as they were productive mediately of personal pleasures.

And in truth Benthamism, as we have seen, except occasionally and inadvertently, recognises only such external obligations to just and benevolent action as we have referred to. The sum of the possible pains to the twelve self-regarding 'interests' originating in the formal or informal (written laws or custom-laws) power of society: the penal and the externally penal is the true and sole fount of obligation.

Hence, we are driven to the conclusion that in Subjective or Intransitive acts the words obligation, authority, conscience, are quite unmeaning, and are simply the equivalents of desirableness, or (if looked at from another point of view), exact calculation; while in Transitive acts (the just and benevolent, or their opposites) obligation simply denotes possible suffering at the hands of our fellow-men. Obligation, in brief, has no concern with morality whatsoever, but properly restricts itself to the sphere of legality.

Could the 'Greatest Happiness' of others *in itself* operate as a permanent external conscience or controlling power, it might serve the purpose in the matter of social acts, and bind communities together; but from the nature of the thing it cannot so operate. The phrase has no meaning until we have settled the individual's greatest happiness; and if that rests on the *Quantitative*, the greatest happiness of man cannot be morally enforced on the individual, because it finds no inner authoritative response: it has only a legal validity, and that always dubious and vacillating.

We should therefore admire the consistency of the thorough-going utilitarians, who, unable to ignore the *fact* of a Moral Sense, as Bentham did, find in it and in what the 'vulgar' call Conscience, only a fictitious entity, an image set up within us by imagination of the social penal forces existing outside us.[1]

---

[1] It is scarcely necessary to say that in estimating Bentham's system we have excluded the *Deontology* from our view, accepting the repudiation of that work by the most competent of Bentham's followers. It is legitimate, however, to refer to it as illustrating the doctrine. The following quotation from vol. ii. p. 132, which may be found in Mr. Burton's *Introduction to Bentham's Works*, will show that we are so far from misrepresenting the true character and consequences of the Benthamite doctrine as to have given a more favourable estimate of it than its professed friends:—'Dream not that men will move their little finger to serve you, unless their advantage in so doing be obvious to them. Men never did so, and never will, while human nature is made of its present materials. But they will desire to serve you when by so doing they can serve themselves; and the occasions on which they can serve themselves by serving you are multitudinous.' See also p. 29 of the *Introduction*. Again, we have the opinion of two distinguished followers of our author (Col. Thompson and Mr. Burton) that '*in nine cases out of ten*' morality yields greater happiness than immorality, although in rare cases it may be otherwise; and, *therefore*, that those who do not choose 'morality,' that is to say, who do not proportion and quantify their lives, commit 'an error and a folly,' and are 'blockheads.' That morality should be rested at all on such a calculation is illustrative of the tenor and consequences of the doctrine.

NEW UTILITARIANISM—MR. MILL.

BENTHAMISM is neither Hobbism nor New-utilitarianism. It stands midway between them. Its errors and defects, exaggerated in the *Deontology*, have during the last forty years been undergoing a quiet revision, which has at last resulted in a new manifesto from the present leader of the school. The inroads which were made on pure Hobbism in the 17th and 18th centuries by Cudworth, Cumberland, Clarke, Shaftesbury, Hutcheson, Butler, and others of less note, are conspicuously visible, as we have shown, in the utilitarian essays of David Hume, and in the ethical system of Bentham himself, notwithstanding his repudiation of a 'Moral Sense' or 'Conscience,' and the contempt with which he treated all speculations proceeding on the assumption that *these* existed. The influence of an advancing psychology, the widening of human sympathies through the artistic and historical literature of the past generation, and to some extent the power of German thought conveyed to us, though in a somewhat blurred form, by Coleridge and Carlyle, have modified the conceptions of all save the extreme positivist left.[1] Mr. Mill, with his large

---

[1] Were I here taking a historical survey of moral doctrine, I could not omit to notice the modification of Paley's system contained in the *Discourse on Ethics*, by William Smith, Barrister-at-Law, published in 1839. In that discourse, which is characterized by much subtlety and eloquence, the system of Paley is translated out of prose into poetry.

receptive as well as active nature, accepts these modifying influences, and in his Essay on Utilitarianism endeavours to reconstruct Benthamism in a spirit adapted to the needs of the time, and with implicit reference to those richer and deeper elements of life which are the inheritance of this generation, and to which the epoch that gave birth to Bentham was comparatively a stranger.

We have found that, according to Bentham, the 'interests' or 'pleasures' of each individual constitute the end of his activity, subject to only one controlling principle, 'The Greatest Happiness on the whole.' In other words, Morality, so far as the individual agent is concerned, is a question of mere quantity, and *might* be determined by caprice or perversity, provided always the agent had regard to that greater mass of possible happiness outside him which is his guide through the perplexities of moral action. Quantitative happiness and an external standard constitute the two main characteristics of the Benthamite ethics. Many as are the merits of Bentham, we do not think that it will be denied by any who derive a knowledge of his argument from his own writings, that, so far as personal morality is concerned, Benthamism cannot consistently put any check on the indulgence of the various pleasures and interests which are enumerated by him, beyond that which the idiosyncracies and circumstances and calculations of the individual may from time to time impose, *until* the gratification of these pleasures and interests hurts the general utility. It must also be admitted that his governing external principle has no *inherent* value or attractiveness to the agent, but *derives its validity and supremacy from the perception of common interests and the pains which the general opinion inflicts on the purely self-regarding citizen;* that, consequently, the only obligation to do the right is to be found in those external sensations of pain and pleasure proceeding *from others*, and affecting for better or worse the numerous susceptibilities and 'interests' of the human constitution as these are detailed by him in his pathological psychology.

Although we find in Mr. Mill such a departure from the strict letter of Benthamism as we should have expected from a man of wider intellectual and imaginative sympathies than the master, we confess that we do not perceive in him a deeper insight into the moral constitution of man, or a clearer apprehension of the scientific defects of the theory which he expounds. The philanthropic zeal which characterized the teacher belongs to his equally distinguished disciple; and this, while giving intensity, also gives narrowness, to the moral vision. The thoughts and desires of both being fixed exclusively on measures tending to the amelioration of society, the equalization of felicities, and the relief of human misery, they take hold of ethical questions only in their relation to the polity of communities, and pay comparatively little attention to the ethics of the individual. Had they started with a more patient analysis of man's nature, and striven to read correctly the moral record written on his heart, they could not, it seems to us, have rested content with the meagre exposition which utilitarianism gives of the ends of human action, of the obligation to pursue those ends, of the doctrine of justice, and of the characteristics of moral energizing. Let us advert to these points in order.

Mr. Mill (and in this he merely heads a host of modern followers) has been compelled to remedy the most conspicuous defect of the Benthamite theory; and explicitly enunciates what Bentham only occasionally alludes to, without allowing for it in his system, viz., the difference in the *quality* of pleasures and pains, and the *natural* superiority of one pleasure to another. He says:—

'It must be admitted, however, that Utilitarian writers in general have placed the superiority of mental over bodily pleasures chiefly in the greater permanency, safety, uncostliness, etc., of the former,—that is, in their circumstantial advantages, rather than in their intrinsic nature. And on all these points utilitarians have fully proved their case; but they might have taken the other, and, as it may be called, higher ground, with entire consistency. It is quite compatible with the principle of utility to recognise the fact, that some *kinds* of pleasure are more desirable and more valuable than others. It would be absurd that, while in estimating all other things quality is considered as well as quantity, the estimation of pleasures should be supposed to depend on quantity alone.'

Again, on page 17, he says :—

'According to the Greatest Happiness principle, the ultimate end with reference to and for the sake of which all other things are desirable (whether we are considering our own good or that of other people), is an existence exempt as far as possible from pain, and as rich as possible in enjoyments both in point of quantity and quality.' . . . 'This being, according to the utilitarian opinion, the end of human action, is necessarily also the standard of morality, which may accordingly be defined the rules and precepts for human conduct, by the observance of which an existence such as has been described might be, to the greatest extent possible, secured to all mankind,' etc.

If this be a true exposition, as we believe it to be, of utilitarian ends, according to the most enlightened conception of these, then Utilitarianism is no longer Benthamism. Quantity, exclusive of Quality, rules in a system *strictly* utilitarian ; and any attempt to define it as being of higher comprehension is a conspicuous departure from the doctrines of the past. Benthamism proper, even although occasionally alluding to the existence of higher interests, has no means of obviating the corollary of its position, viz., that two lower interests must overbalance *one* higher interest ; and if (for some special reason) not *two*, then three or four. Were there any doubt as to the correctness of this estimate of the utilitarian theory *of ends*, it would be removed by a consideration of the theory of obligation which supports it, and which is drawn solely from the influence which *external* sanctions exercise on the quantity of the personal pleasures and pains of the moral agent. It is further confirmed by the fact that Bentham, while tabulating the springs of action, and endeavouring elsewhere to lay a basis of ethical psychology for his system of ends and sanctions, never takes up the most important of all the psychological questions which could have come within his range—the *relative* importance of interests, in any other than a quantitative sense.

Accordingly, we gladly note this new modification of the utilitarian theory of human life. At one bound we are carried out of utilitarianism proper into a species of ill-defined eudæmonism, which has no small affinity to the principles of Shaftesbury and Hutcheson. There is now an explicitly avowed gradation among felicities, and the 'Greatest Happiness' theory is at once transformed into the '*Highest* Happiness' theory. Accordingly, for a moment we imagine ourselves on the firm ground of a subjective system of ethics, and begin to turn the pages hastily in the hope of meeting with a new and improved table of the Benthamite 'interests,' containing some touchstone of quality, as well as a measure of quantity. Instead of this, we are introduced merely to an inadequate re-statement of the doctrine of David Hume, whose view of the eudæmonistic theory, spite of its want of thorough systematizing, was the result of a much more thorough analysis than any that has yet appeared on the utilitarian side. We expect to find removed the confusion of the Benthamite doctrine, which, losing sight of *individual* morality altogether, raises the standard of the 'Greatest happiness of the greatest number,' without defining wherein the true inner happiness of each individual of that number consists, thereby leaving us to find a motive or obligation to right action in considerations purely external. Great, therefore, is our disappointment to find that Hume's advanced position has been here overlooked, and that Mr. Mill has omitted to take advantage of his predecessor's distinctions to give fixedness, decision, and consistency to what is little more than a reproduction of the more thoroughly excogitated eudæmonism of the Scottish sceptic.

The end as well as the criterion of the individual's action is, according to Hume, the highest happiness of the individual; the end of all social acts is the happiness of society: and that which constitutes private and public acts, moral or immoral, that is to say, approvable or censurable, is their conformity to these standards respectively. No sooner has Mr. Mill seemed to seize this distinction than it slips from his grasp, either in consequence of a half-conscious surmise of the difficulties into which it might lead him when he should enter on the question of ethical psychology, or from a habit of mind acquired by a too exclusive converse with only one of the two parallel lines of philosophical thought which have marked the history of the world.

He has just caught a view of the principle of subjective eudæmonism when he leaps aside; and in the illustrations which follow, and in which he combats some of the 'vulgar' prejudices against the 'Greatest Happiness' theory, he allows at one time the individual happiness, at another the general happiness to dominate over his argument. The martyr (to use his own illustration), even in renouncing life and courting a painful death, foregoes happiness of many kinds, not for the sake of a *personal* happiness which more than outweighs them all, but for the sake of the happiness of his fellow-creatures. Now, to our thinking, the martyr performed the supreme act of Rightness; but why? Because he loved his fellow-men so that he preferred to dare all suffering in order to bear testimony to a principle of human conduct fraught with happiness to man here and hereafter. And further, because he loved the Source of all Truth so, that to have been unfaithful to the particular truth for which he daringly witnessed would have been a severance of his inner life from its God, and a wilful exile of himself into a region of spiritual death. The pang of such a separation would have been deeper than all pains which man could inflict: nay, perhaps the joy of conscious union with God was so intense, that, like an ancient Stoic, he could not admit that the inflictions of men were even worthy of the name of pain. If this be a true interpretation, so far as it goes, of the motives which sustain the martyr,—namely, love to man and love to God,—these motives are subjective. Psychologically speaking, he has sacrificed all present and future felicities of this life in order to testify to his supreme felicity in the sentiments of Good-will to man and of Love of God. But Mr. Mill is shy of any such conclusion: he looks outside the martyr's sentiments only, and although finding his motive in the general diffusion of happiness, he does not seem to see that as a motive this must have been barren of all possible fruit, except in so far as it stirred in the martyr's own bosom the joy of a supreme act of Love. So shy, indeed, is Mr. Mill of any other interpretation of the martyr's act, that he (naïvely it seems to us) asks this question, 'Would it (the sacrifice) be made if he thought that his renunciation of happiness for himself would produce no fruit for any of his fellow-creatures, but to make their lot like his, and place them also in the condition of persons who have renounced happiness?' The answer is, taking happiness in the sense which Mr. Mill's argument gives it, 'Yes; not only for himself would he "count it all joy" thus to suffer, but he would gladly call *all* men to a like glorious destiny.' It is the treatment of such practical questions as these which reveals the inherent weakness of utilitarianism, and shows that, even in the hands of one who readily admits variety and gradation in human felicities, the doctrine is so interpenetrated with error as to render but sorry help to those who desire to look into the labyrinths and recesses of man's moral nature.

Lest by any chance the frequent employment of the word 'happiness,' and its occasional use in a connexion in which it can only mean the happiness of the individual agent, should mislead the reader, Mr. Mill hastens to say that 'the only self-renunciation which it (the utilitarian morality) applauds is devotion to the happiness, or to some of the means of happiness, of others; either of mankind collectively, or of individuals within the limits imposed by the collective interests of mankind;' and with still greater emphasis he adds, 'I must again repeat what the assailants of Utilitarianism seldom have the justice to acknowledge, that the happiness which forms the utilitarian standard of what is right in conduct is not the agent's own happiness, but that of all concerned' (that is to say, of humanity). Thus after having raised our hopes by distinguishing *kinds* of human felicity, he fails to furnish us with any scientific, graduated classification of these felicities, and quickly losing sight of the subjective ground on which he *had* for a moment taken his stand when enunciating the qualitative element, he falls back into the old Benthamite position, and offers us the '*general utility*' as the standard of each and every act. Accordingly, while we gladly, under Mr. Mill's guidance, translate the phrase, 'the greatest happiness of the greatest number,' into 'the highest happiness of the greatest number,' we find that, even in his good company, we still find ourselves furnished with only an *external* standard of right, which can have only external sanctions. At best, and under the most favourable interpretation which can be given of it, an objective eudæmonism is all that is offered in place of the Benthamite utilitarianism.

Nay, on close examination we find that the seeming gift is, after all, only an empty and illusory phrase. For, how can I ascertain the highest happiness of a community, that is to say, of a number of men whom accident or design has brought within each other's influence, without first knowing wherein consists the happiness of each man as man—not of this, that, or the other particular individual, but of man. Having ascertained this, either I as an agent am to be guided by this ascertained happiness, which now becomes my *individual happiness* and my duty, even in those acts which affect others; or (and this is the sole alternative) I am to allow the happiness of the majority to be the governing principle of my actions, *simply because* the majority have concurred in thinking this to be my duty.

That this is felt by Mr. Mill to be the alternative, appears from his anxiety to take measures for *creating* in man a *habit* of mind in harmony with the general interest of the whole. This is to be done by so constructing the State machinery 'that laws and social arrangements should place the happiness or (as speaking practically it may be called) the interest of every individual as nearly as possible in harmony with the interest of the whole;' and secondly, by deliberately making use of education and opinion to establish in the mind of every individual an indissoluble association between his own happiness and the good of the whole, so that not only he may be unable to conceive the possibility of happiness to himself consistently with conduct opposed to the general good, but also that a direct impulse to promote the general good may be in every individual one of the habitual motives of action. Now, cleverly as this doctrine is propounded, it will be found, when narrowly inspected, to be simply a re-statement of pure Benthamism, and even to contain diluted Hobbism. The New-utilitarianism, accordingly, notwithstanding its more explicit enunciation of quality in felicities, thus exposes its inability to find for itself any scientific basis save that provided by Bentham, unless it moves a step further, and wholly identifies itself with subjective ethics. The action of the State, according to Mr. Mill, is to endow men with a kind of factitious conscience; and men will *further* be taught that they are consulting their own interests in yielding to the general opinion of the community. They are, in point of fact, to be so instructed that they will see that by giving away a little now, they will secure a return of much at some future day, through the operation of that very rule which they are perhaps grudgingly obeying. In short, to use the words of David Hume, if men will conform their conduct to the principle of utility, they will 'find their account in it.' This is surely to exaggerate Benthamism; for, when fairly estimated, what is this but to say that the supreme standard of conduct is a man's *own* individual felicity, *excluding benevolence* from among the number of his felicities,—a doctrine which Bentham would never have sanctioned. At best it places benevolence on a level with felicities of other kinds, and thereby brings us back into the region of pure quantitative ethics.

If Mr. Mill should reply (as from one passage we infer that he would) that a portion, and a large portion, of the happiness of each moral agent arises out of the gratification of the instinct of Good-will, and that the gratification of this instinct, as well as of other and lower felicities, is indissolubly bound up with 'an impulse to promote the general good,' this is simply to utter the identical proposition, that the gratification of the instinct of Good-will is bound up with the gratification of the instinct of Good-will: and if we then go on to ask, 'Why should I, a free agent, gratify my good-will more than my self-will?' the only additional inducement which can be offered to me is, as we have already indicated, that by so doing I secure a reversion of many other felicities in addition to the present possession of the felicity of benevolence. I thus, as it were, put out to usury the capital of my benevolence, and, while enjoying the luxury of possessing it, I, at the same time, secure a large dividend out of the general stock of felicities. It is because this is dimly felt to be in the long-run an intellectual calculation—an arithmetical summation—that utilitarians urge so vehemently the importance of forming the opinions and mental habits of the people; and it is because it is an intellectual calculation that a man may be not only excused for working the sum in a different way from Bentham or Mr. Mill, but be held *morally blameless* if he chooses to direct his life on the principle of pursuing only the self-regarding pleasures; unless it be maintained that that man is blameworthy who declines to accept the prevalent opinion of a community as Moral law.

If Mr. Mill, in evasion of the grosser consequences of his doctrine, should fall back on the glimpse of subjective eudæmonism which he enjoyed when speaking of the quality as opposed to the quantity of human felicities, and should affirm that the moral agent above referred to is blameworthy because he has refused to follow after that felicity which is the supreme and governing felicity of a normal nature, we rejoin by inquiring, 'How is this ascertained?' Should Mr. Mill meet us, as in one place he substantially does, with the reply, 'By the common consent of all men who have experienced this as well as the other felicities;' we then lead him to this unexpected conclusion, that inasmuch as it is by a comparison of our inner feelings that we detect certain *qualities* in the various felicities of which we are susceptible, and inasmuch as that felicity, which reasoning consciousness tells us is the highest, is also the felicity which, *ipso facto*, and by Divine right, is entitled to control all other felicities, and be the end of human action,—we say, since these things are so, the standard of Morality may be felicity, but it is the felicity of Man—subjective felicity, subjective in relation to the reason of Man as Man, and that in *this* subjective felicity each individual finds revealed his own true Duty and Happiness. In this subjective eudæmonism new-utilitarianism must end, or it must revert to the pure Benthamite doctrine, which *ultimately*—if not also explicitly as in the case of Hobbes—rests the supreme and guiding principle of human conduct on the general opinion or will of the community, and enforces it by the pains and pleasures which the community holds in its hand, supporting it by certain additional reversionary advantages which arise from obeying the current law, customary or written. Our hope and our belief is, that it is in a subjective eudæmonism that new-utilitarianism is destined to issue; and further, that in such a system of subjective eudæmonism, based on a thorough analysis of emotional states, and of their association with the sentiment of Law and Duty, is to be found the reconciliation of the long opposed schools of ethical thought.

Great as are the self-contradictions and confusions characteristic of this new-utilitarianism in its treatment of the standard or criterion of rightness in conduct, these defects are still more conspicuous in its treatment of the *sanctions* of rightness. It has been necessary, in following Mr. Mill's line of argument, to associate this question of obligation to some extent with that of the separate and prior question of the criterion of rightness; but the question itself is one which demands, and will repay, separate consideration. The question, '*Why* is a man to adapt his acts to the promotion of the collective interests of the community?' is the crucial question of ethics, and tests, more than any other, the soundness of ethical analysis.

It is not to be doubted that Mr. Mill is right in thinking that that class of obligatory considerations distinguished as *external* sanctions, belongs to the utilitarian morality quite as much as to any other possible system; but the same cannot be said of the *internal* sanctions. There is some vagueness in the treatment of this question of sanctions in Bentham's hands; and we do not find that Mr. Mill has done anything to remove it. An external sanction, in the strictest sense, is a force operating on a man *ab extra*, inducing or compelling him to do a certain act. These sanctions generally admit of being referred to one of two classes—the sanction of the Approbation of man, or the sanction of the Approbation of God. But it is evident that these two sanctions may be efficacious in two ways, which we may distinguish as the direct and indirect, or the primary and secondary. Bentham rests their force on the consequences which may flow from them, beneficial or detrimental, to other (and as we should say, lower) 'interests,' than the love of the approbation of man and the love of the approbation of God *in themselves*. The same tendency exhibits itself in the majority of utilitarian writers. Now, while we admit the force of these secondary or indirect consequences of sanctions originating *ab extra*, it is not to be denied that the mere displeasure of our fellow-men, and still more the displeasure of the Almighty, are *in themselves* a ground of moral pain, just as their opposites are sources of a high felicity. As was to be expected from Mr. Mill's recognition of the qualitative element in ends and motives, the *direct* or primary operation of the external sanctions also finds a place in his system, although it is not drawn out as a distinguishing characteristic of New-utilitarianism, but merely indicated in a general way, thus : '[The external sanctions] are the hope of favour and the fear of displeasure from our fellow-creatures or from the Ruler of the universe, along with whatever we may have of sympathy or affection for them, or of love and awe of Him inclining us to do His will *independently of selfish consequences.*' This, along with other passages, may be accepted as an intimation by Mr. Mill that he includes, among moral sanctions, the primary pains and pleasures of human and divine approbation as well as the secondary or derivative. If this be so, it is of importance to remark the conclusion to which this leads in the department of ethical psychology ; namely, that man has an instinctive or innate sentiment of love of Approbation. If we add this to the instinctive sentiment of Good-will, which we, some pages back, deduced as a necessary consequence from Mr. Mill's doctrine of ends, we have the satisfaction of finding that Mr. Mill's ethical system, if fully exhibited, would begin with claiming for man certain sentiments as instinctive or innate. If we are right, Mr. Mill's New-utilitarianism requires revision, and must ultimately take the form of an explicit subjective eudæmonism ; if we are wrong, much of what might be called the virtuous and sentimental halo in which he continues to envelop the bald doctrine of objective utility is shown to be no longer the native and self-produced atmosphere of his doctrine, but a bright reflection caught from the glory of another and a better system.

Let us now pass to the question of internal sanctions, that is to say, sanctions that *originate* within, for all sanctions are ultimately in their effect internal. Mr. Mill's internal sanctions—and herein there is a wide departure from the position of the Old-utilitarianism and a large addition to its moral resources—may be summed up as—(1.) The subjective feeling of duty; (2.) A conviction of the community and harmony of our aims and interests with those of our fellow-men. The latter is the *ultimate* sanction of the 'Greatest-happiness' morality, the feeling of 'duty' being associated with it more or less closely according to the clearness of the apprehension or the education of the individual agent. Now, if we consider this ultimate internal sanction or inner binding force, we find that it may be analysed into two elements : *first*, an intellectual perception on the part of each individual member of society, that his own interests can be promoted only if subordinated to the promotion of the general interest, which is a merely prudential, calculating, selfish, and quantitative consideration, and throws us back into the crudest form of Utilitarianism; *secondly*, a feeling that his happiness is imperfect, unless attained with due regard to the *superior* claims of the happiness of the community of which he forms a part. Mr. Mill, in his argument, does not carry out this distinction; on the contrary, the two elements of his ultimate sanction are so inextricably intertwined as to lead to a painful confusion in the exposition. The former of the two elements we at once set aside as already disposed of in the consideration of right ends, and as unworthy even of New-utilitarianism, much more of any subjective theory of obligation. The second element seems to be seized by Mr. Mill in those passages in which he refers to the basis of 'natural sentiment, which lies at the foundation of the ultimate utilitarian sanction.' 'This firm foundation,' he says, 'is that of the social feelings of mankind; the desire to be in unity with our fellow-creatures, which is already a powerful principle in human nature, and happily one of those which tend to become stronger, even without express inculcation from the influences of advancing civilisation.' And further on he says, 'Whatever amount of this feeling a person has, he is urged by the strongest motives, both of interest and of sympathy, to demonstrate it, and to the utmost of his power encourage it in others:' 'The smallest germs of the feeling are laid hold of and encouraged by the contagion of sympathy and the influences of education; and a complete web of corroborative association is woven round it by the powerful agency of the external sanctions.' From all which it follows, that the basis of the ultimate sanction, and, consequently, the ultimate sanction itself of the Right, is, according to Mr. Mill, neither more nor less than the Social Feeling which is instinctive in man, as in many other animals, and which, apart from ulterior considerations of interest, forbids his ever permanently regarding himself as a mere unit, and compels him to regard himself as one of a community, and to have supreme regard to that community in all that he does.

But in so far as this is a *feeling*, it is neither more nor less than sympathy of man with man—a sympathy causing him to court the company of his kind, and to understand their pleasures and their pains through his own. We admit the soundness of this sympathetic basis so far, and recognise in it a foundation on which skilful politicians may, in the course of generations, erect a superstructure of regard for the interests of others; nay more, of *supreme* regard for those interests. Without this basis of natural sympathy, it would be impossible to speak intelligently or intelligibly of the *common* interest, or show how a sovereign regard for it re-acts in a thousand ways on the interests of the individual who is required to take it as his ethical standard. Having served this purpose, however, its power is exhausted. It gives the politician facilities for bringing *external* sanctions to bear on his fellow-men, whether these be the external sanctions which affect his sentiments, or those which affect personal felicities of a lower quality. Mr. Mill's instinctive sympathetic social sense renders all this possible; but having done this it can do no more. To attribute more to it, and to elevate it into *the* inner sanction of the Right, is to mistake the nature of sympathy. Through sympathy we understand what is in others, and we may also be drawn towards them because of their likeness to ourselves; but no movement of active interest in their welfare, not even a distant regard for it, could arise without an inner moving force—the force of love, good-will, or benevolence.

Does Mr. Mill mean to convey all this as implied in the sympathetic social sense? He certainly hovers round the active side of the sentiment, as if he would fain appropriate it as the ultimate binding force of utilitarianism. If it be not implicitly contained in Mr. Mill's social sense, then it is manifestly vain to talk of there being any *inner* sanction of utilitarianism, or any ultimate sanction whatsoever, other than those external sanctions, primary and derivative, of which we have already spoken. If, on the other hand, the active sentiment of good-will be implicitly contained in the social sense, then the ultimate sanction of the 'Greatest-Happiness' morality is the inner force which *stimulates us to achieve for ourselves the subjective felicity of an active good-will,* and which inflicts pain if this other-regarding sentiment be superseded by the self-regarding motives. Disguise it as we may, the force which ultimately and chiefly impels us to shape our conduct with a supreme regard to the general well-being, is this subjective felicity of an active good-will. Does it not follow, then, that our ethical psychology must recognise in man an innate sentiment of good-will, and that inasmuch as this sentiment is the chief motive-power influencing the individual's acts, the *satisfaction of this sentiment is also the purpose or end of the individual's activity?* To ask even the New-utilitarian explicitly to admit this, would be to require him to substitute subjective ends for objective ends as the standard of rightness in acting. But should he do so, he need fear no detriment to the interests of humanity; for while, among conflicting motives and ends, good-will, as motive and end, is to reign supreme, it is manifest that the moment the individual agent has achieved inner harmony and moral unity by the identification of his will with the other-regarding sentiment, his next business is to see that he does not fail of his purpose and that the benevolent activity is not abortive. His *act* has an outer history in the future, no less than his energizing has had a subjective history in the past. He must see to it that the suggestions of good-will are truly so designed as to achieve their objective end—the highest happiness of mankind. His energizing has been moral, right, praiseworthy, good. He must make sure that the results of the energizing are apt, fit, wise, intelligent. To discover this, he is again necessarily thrown back on subjective ethics, and is compelled to form for himself a scheme, however crude, of man's nature and of his true good.

Were New-utilitarianism once distinctly to take up this subjective eudæmonistic position, a great step would be made towards a reconciliation with the Intuitional school. For the latter school, when adequately represented, does not omit from its system the external sanctions of the right, or the inner sanction of felicity in acting in conformity to the right. Its chief deviation from a subjective eudæmonism is to be found in its doctrine of an inner law as at once, arbitrarily and without regard to felicity, discriminating the Right, and authoritatively imposing the obligation to do it.

Mr. Mill's chapter on sanctions is followed by one which aims at giving the *proof* of the utilitarian doctrine. The argument runs thus: Questions about ends are questions about things desirable. The Utilitarian doctrine is, that Happiness is *alone* desirable as an end, all other desirable things being only means to that end. That Happiness is an end, can be proved only by appealing to the consciousness of each, and showing that each desires it for himself. If individual happiness is desirable as an end, it follows that the aggregate happiness, or the happiness of the sum of individuals, is desirable. But Happiness, individual and aggregate, is not merely *an* end—it is the sole final end. It is true that virtue is also desired as an end in a certain sense; but this and certain other seeming ends are in truth only means to the final end, *happiness*. Virtue is desired as a part of happiness, and as a means to it. 'Whatever,' he says, 'is desired otherwise than as a means to some end beyond itself, and ultimately to happiness, is desired as itself a *part* of happiness, and is not desired for itself, until it has become so. Those who desire Virtue for its own sake, desire it either because the consciousness of it is a pleasure, or because the consciousness of being without it is a pain, or for both reasons united.' The validity of the proof depends on its being a fact that human nature is so constituted as to desire nothing which is not either a part of happiness, or a means of happiness. For evidence of this, we can only appeal to the consciousness of men, which will respond that 'to desire anything except in proportion as the idea of it is pleasant, is a physical and metaphysical impossibility.'

We set aside for the time Mr. Mill's notion of virtue. Like his notion of duty (to which also we here only make a passing allusion), it is derived from a vague and confused popular interpretation of popular terms. It would be easy to show that in the case of the latter term, his notion is as inadequate as in the case of the former it is a misapprehension. We content ourselves with asking, 'Assuming the validity of the above argument, what has been proved?' That Happiness is the sole desirable end of the individual's action, and by consequence of the action of the sum of individuals, that is to say, of each of all individuals; the latter part of the proposition being simply a larger statement of the former part. Without entering into the logomachy of happiness ends, and virtue ends, and duty ends, we would take up Mr. Mill's own position for a moment, and ask, whether the above propositions do distinctly enounce that the final end, and, *therefore*, the ultimate test or criterion of rightness for each individual agent, is the individual's Happiness? If this be so—and, with the best intentions, we cannot see that Mr. Mill's argument admits of any other interpretation—we find ourselves quite away from the ground of utilitarianism, as again and again insisted on by himself, and thrown into the arms of a subjective eudæmonism. Mr. Mill, in truth, hovers on the confines of this region from the first page of his book to the last, and consequently, in his rehabilitation of Benthamism, he has been led into manifold assumptions in argument, and inconsistencies of language; but now he seems to have fairly crossed the border, and to find himself permanently settled in a new region—the region of subjective ethics.

And yet, blind to the true significance of his own utterances, he remains so hampered by the Benthamite net-work which he wove round his intellect in his youth, that he is betrayed in one portion of his argument into defining the happiness which is the end of life and of morality as an aggregate of many pleasurable ingredients, thereby losing sight of the *moral* question altogether, and identifying *happiness as a test of action* with happiness in the vulgar acceptation—a resultant, pleasurable self-complacency. Why, even according to his most explicit statements elsewhere, this is not a true definition even of the end and criterion of those acts of a man which directly or indirectly affect others ; for the happiness of others by which conduct is to be tested is not *such* quantitative happiness—which would give us a system of pure hedonism—but the *highest* happiness of *others*, even though the attaining of this should cause the agent to subject both himself and others to grievous toils and pains.

When next we approach Mr. Mill's doctrine of Justice, which occupies a large portion of his book, we find ourselves going over again the argumentative ground already traversed ; but on this branch of the ethical question, if the Old-utilitarian position was strong, that of the New-utilitarian is almost impregnable. Admitting this, and also perceiving that New-utilitarians and Intuitionalists are in this practical region substantially at one, we are naturally led to inquire into the grounds of this sudden reconciliation. The reconciliation is accounted for by the fact that the Intuitionalist has here left behind him *moral* questions, as he rightly understands morality, and is concerned solely with those overt and transitive acts which affect the well-being, moral and physical, of his fellow-men. Accordingly, he can cordially unite with the

New-utilitarian in the objective end of all transitive acts, and with him recognise the 'highest' happiness of the community as the criterion of these. In this region of what might be called distributive morality, there is no conflict. In truth, were the utilitarian but once for all clearly to see that his discussions for the most part do not revolve round the questions of ethics strictly speaking, but have to do only with political ethics, which concerns itself with the distribution of felicities, the way would be cleared for the mutual understanding of the opposing schools of philosophy.

The doctrine of Justice, we have said, in its *objective* relations can call forth no reclaiming statement from Intuitionalists, as we understand intuitionalism: but when the question necessarily arises, 'What is the sentiment of Justice?' psychologically speaking, and 'What are the sanctions of Just willing?' the conflict is resumed with as keen hostility as ever. Mr. Mill tells us that 'whatever is moral' in the sentiment of Justice arises 'from the idea of expediency'—a position which carries him back as far as Hobbes, and far away from the subjective theory towards which in other parts of his essay he seems to be approximating.

To enter upon this large question with due regard to its importance would involve very many pages of discussion, and has in its chief aspects been anticipated elsewhere.[1] We content ourselves, therefore, with pointing out that both the Old and the New-utilitarian rest the interpretation and obligation of the just act, as

[1] *Philosophy of Ethics*, chapter on Justice.

of all morality, on external sanctions. The Old-utilitarian finds its obligatoriness in sanctions which originate in the will of others than the agent. The New-utilitarian adds, or at least may consistently add, to those outward penal sanctions, the inner reproaches of conscience, although he has not yet ventured to define what he means by these. This inadequate view of the obligation of Justice compels both schools of utilitarians to look persistently only at the *negative* aspect of the question, and to offer a definition of the sentiment of *Injustice* for a definition of the sentiment of *Justice*—practically identifying both with what is only a partial definition of the former, namely, *the desire to inflict retaliatory punishment*.[1] This negative aspect of the sentiment is certainly chronologically prior in the experience of man to the positive. But though it is thus the beginning, it is not therefore the source or fountain of the positive sentiment.

It follows also, from the view of obligation taken by both old and new utilitarians, that the specific and differentiating characteristic of *a* right or 'rights' which enters into both the notion and the sentiment of Justice, is supposed to be adequately indicated by saying that it is resolvable into 'an apprehended hurt to some assignable person or persons on the one hand, and a desire to punish on the other.'[2] The *whole* sentiment of Justice, therefore, of which the notion or feeling of *a right* forms confessedly only a part, is thus represented as differing from the latter solely in

[1] Pp. 76-78 of Mill's *Utilitarianism*. [2] *Ibid.* p. 79.

the fact of the superinduction of the social feeling. But inasmuch as the apprehension of a hurt to some assignable person involves the sympathy of the spectator, and inasmuch as sympathy, according to Mr. Mill, constitutes the essence of the social feeling—it follows that in New-utilitarianism the notion of *a right* in no respect differs from the sentiment of Justice itself. Thus the figure which it was necessary to add to the notion of *a right* in order to complete the sentiment of Justice is at best a cipher without a multiplying power.

In conclusion, we can assure Mr. Mill that it is no necessary part of the creed of Intuitionalism (although the generalities in which its defenders too often indulge justify his criticism) to hold that 'Justice is wholly independent of utility, and is a standard *per se* which the mind can recognise by simple introspection of itself.' We no more believe this than that the terms Right, Duty, Conscience defy analysis, and are invested with a sacredness which should prohibit it.

The exposition which we have endeavoured to give of utilitarianism as advocated by Mr. Mill, brief though it has necessarily been, will suffice at least to suggest the relation of his doctrine to past and present theories; and if, in our estimate of it, we cannot admit that it possesses so consistent and thoroughgoing a character as the parent utilitarianism of Bentham, it is gratifying to find that its deficiencies in respect of logical precision and inner consistency are due to a deeper sensibility and a wider reach of thought than were characteristic of the older doctrine, and consequently give good promise of an approach to that non-personal subjective sentimental eudæmonism in which are to be found, we believe, the elements of the reconciliation of a strife which has lasted for more than two thousand years.

PROFESSOR BAIN'S UTILITARIANISM.[1]

AMONG other remarks which indicate the dubious attitude assumed by Mr. Mill towards utilitarianism, is a footnote on p. 73 of his essay, in which he speaks in terms of strong laudation of Mr. Bain's ethical views. A more careful consideration of these, especially in their connexion with Mr. Bain's *Dissertations and Notes on Paley*, which are in perfect harmony with more recent expressions of opinion, would have shown Mr. Mill that, except in the recognition of Honour and the Virtues as existing in some artistic region of man's nature, Mr. Bain out-Bentham's Bentham, and revives the very doctrines which Mr. Mill has laboured to qualify and amend. Were it not, indeed, for this reactionary character of Mr. Bain's writings—reactionary as against advanced utilitarianism itself—it might not be necessary here to exhibit their tendencies.

'To illustrate further the nature of right,' says Mr. Bain, 'we would remark that obligation implies *punishment*. Where a penalty cannot be inflicted, there is no effective obligation; and in cases where, although rules have been violated, punishment is not

---

[1] As the basis of our remarks on Mr. Bain, we have taken the *Dissertations and Notes on Paley*, collating these, however, with his work on the *Emotions and the Will*.

considered proper, obligation is virtually denied. We find, for example, that there is no disposition to punish men for not being benevolent; and, therefore, we must presume that benevolence is not held to be a universal and indispensable duty. . . . Punishment means the infliction of positive pain or evil in amount proportioned to the degree and the continuance of the offence.'[1]

This theory of obligation or moral law contains implicitly Mr. Bain's theory of morality. By permitting the question of obligation to override the question of moral ends, and, consequently, of the standard of the right, he has, in our opinion, introduced further confusion into ethical science. This confusion he has succeeded in overcoming, in so far as the consistency of his own thought is concerned, by giving a special and arbitrary definition to the term obligation. If that only is a matter of obligation which society compels a man to do under pain of suffering, and which his personal and physical security compels him to do under a similar penalty, it follows that morality proper is confined within the sphere of the penal; and that all acts other than those which are so essential to personal and social security as to fall under the notice of the police, lie outside the moral, the right, the obligatory, and require to be arranged under some new name.

Ends of Action.—Accordingly, when we turn to the dissertation on the ends of action, we find these

[1] *Notes on Paley,* p. 86.

classified as ends of primary, secondary, and what we may call tertiary[1] morality, according to the extent of the obligatoriness. *Primary* morality includes all those acts which bear so directly on personal and social Security as to be subjects of legislation, written or unwritten, and which are consequently of full obligation. *Secondary* morality embraces such acts of benevolence as exceed the legal demands of society, and are of less obligation. Lastly, such acts of nobleness, self-sacrifice, purity, heroism as call forth our admiration, in consequence of their being akin to the beautiful and sublime in nature and art, may be included under the head of *tertiary*, or, as it might also be denominated, artistic morality.

Let us shortly look at these Moral ends in their order.

The following quotations convey with sufficient clearness Mr. Bain's doctrine of Primary morality :—

'Man has, under an instinct of self-preservation, the care of his own being, or the maintenance of his bodily existence, with the provision of all things essential thereto.' . . . 'The rules and maxims of bodily prudence come to be improved and refined upon as intelligence is expanded, and, at the same time, new motives of obedience are brought into play.' . . . 'The end of prudential morality may, therefore, be assumed to be the preservation and the pleasure of the individual.' . . . 'The uniform practice

---

[1] This term *tertiary* is not employed by Mr. Bain, but it is implied in his classifications, and the employment of it helps to bring out his meaning.

observed among human beings of forming associations among themselves, and living in mutual dependence, puts a new face upon the necessities, and therefore upon the conduct and duties of individual men and women.' . . . 'An enlargement of the circle of pleasures and pains, and of the motive to action that these furnish, is the consequence of man's sociability; moreover, the mere necessities of life, the means of bodily sustenance and security, are better obtained by social co-operation.' . . . Thus it gradually comes about that 'the [instinctive] revulsion against *personal* harm is equally excited by a wrong done to the *society* that protects the person and secures its means of subsistence. A man must no more sin against the order of the society that he lives among, than against his daily bread and nightly shelter. The duties of obedience and social rule are duties of self-preservation, and have always been felt as such where we human beings have been drawn into social unions.' . . . 'Hence obedience to Law and the social virtues being indispensable to man's very existence, have the highest degree of obligation and imperative force that any consideration in the whole compass of being can possess.'

The end and motive of primary morality then is the comfort and security of the individual agent. Even those acts which he does nominally for society are done in reality *for himself.* There are, it is true, many classes of social acts which are held to be imperative, which do not seem at first sight to fall under the head of primary morality, and which, therefore, have not the strongest claim on our obedience. Such, for example, are those acts indicated by the word *Integrity*. But, according to Mr. Bain, if we look closer at the matter, we shall find that this virtue is necessary to the social well-being and to the progress of civilisation. 'It may be proved to have its roots in the highest necessities and most salient benefits of human life.' *Integrity*, then, is to be cultivated for the sake of the social security: and as we have seen that the social security is to govern our acts, *because* it is merely a disguised *personal* security, it follows that integrity is to be practised because it promotes the individual's personal security and comfort.

But there are other virtues, such as Benevolence, Purity, Justice, Obedience to law. What of these? They too, it seems, derive their *obligatory* character from their bearing on the social security and comfort; and 'the recognised duties and virtues of the ordinary morality' derive their validity (in so far, we presume, as they may or can be legitimately enforced) from their contributing to 'the ends bodily preservation and social security;' that is to say, really and ultimately, the *comfort and security of the individual acting*. That all the virtues, in so far as they belong to the primary morality, are only an indirect means of obtaining comfort and security for the individual who is called upon to practise them, is an inevitable consequence of Mr. Bain's reasoning. In truth, it constitutes his reasoning,—the thin disguise of utility and social felicity being occasionally thrown over the bare skeleton of the lowest form of selfism. It is at once manifest that this is an extreme form of the Benthamite utilitarianism. The high standard of the 'Greatest Happiness on the whole,' as the ground of obligation for practising social duties and social virtues, and as giving to society its right to inflict penalties, is lost sight of. The development is a natural one; it is the fruit of a logical mind employed upon the Benthamite doctrine in all its logical hardness, and endeavouring to give it scientific and systematic exposition. In the effort to do so, there is an inevitable relapse into Hobbism. That this is so, must be apparent to any one who can see that the primary ground of any social duty must be either calculating selfism, or sentiment, or law; either an extended and refined personal prudence, the exhibition and gratification of a specific characteristic of rational minds, or obedience to duty.

Obligation.—If we have correctly explained Mr. Bain's theory of primary moral ends and the grounds of obligation, we have, by implication, given expression to his standard or criterion of rightness. *That act is right which is calculated to advance the individual agent's personal security as the member of a community.* Mr. Bain may decline to accept this inference: it is nevertheless correct. The criterion of rightness is thus brought back to a personal or subjective standard, and society is deprived of all *right* to impose primary morality, except in so far as it derives it from its *might*. The majority, in respect of power (not necessarily of numbers) *originates* duties and virtues, and authoritatively declares them. In other words, the State is the source of right; and thus we again encounter the crudest Hobbism.

Mr. Bain would probably here direct attention to the fact, that under primary morality he speaks only of those classes of acts which society has a right to enforce by legal penalties; and that in his secondary morality the same virtues which have been treated in their primary and binding character reappear as qualities not 'absolutely binding,' but laudable and desirable in each and all, and as being, *in some sense*, obligatory. The answer to this is to be found in his own treatment of the subject. On pages 15 and 88 of his edition of Paley, it will be found that of all the virtues, Benevolence (as a form of tenderness) alone comes before us as having a quasi-obligation. Even of it he says, ' that actions of pure benevolence [that is to say, exceeding the legal or enforceable demand] do not come within the scope of obligatory duty, but are in a manner left open to the choice of the individual.' It is true that on more than one occasion he feels himself hard pushed to hold his ground, and under the influence of this pressure, or, it may be, of intellectual confusion, he introduces benevolence as a *primary* duty; as when he says (p. 6), ' The affections and sympathies felt by a man towards his fellows may be a source of disinterested regard to their interests in common with his own.' Again (p. 11), 'The virtue of humanity or benevolence commends itself as being the offspring of one of the most powerful and luxurious of our constitutional impulses; namely, the emotion of natural tenderness, which enters into and sweetens all the relations of mutual dependence.' Further, at a later stage of his argument, when treating of the Secondary morality, that is to say, of the exercise of a kind of overplus of benevolence, or what we might fitly call gratuitous acts of good-will, he, in despair of finding any ground of real *obligation* for enforcing a duty so fraught with good consequences, slips into the statement not explicitly made, but rather evaded in the treatment of the Primary morality, viz., ' As our primary morality would have (*sic*) to include the cardinal virtue of benevolence or humanity, we might,' etc. Notwithstanding, however, these misplaced and inadvertent observations, we find not only in the passages already quoted, but pervading the whole argument, the proposition that benevolence falls under *primary* morality, that is to say, is obligatory, only in so far as it contributes to personal security and comfort. 'Every human being has a positive interest in it. We are all liable to fall into dependent situations; *therefore*,' etc. Moreover, as a motive for acting with benevolence, we are told that we have to lay up store not only of worldly good, but, with a view to possible exigencies, we 'must lay up a *character* that will sustain the pressure of evil days.' Accordingly we conclude that benevolence enters into enforceable or primary morality on the same terms as integrity, of which it is said, 'If there be any cases where a breach of integrity can produce no evil consequences of any kind, either relating to the bonds of society, retarding the cause of truth, inducing a habit of unveracity, or exciting suspicion or distrust, there would scarcely exist any conceivable motive for enforcing the practice of this virtue.' So of Purity, Justice, and so forth. We are accordingly compelled to regard Benevolence and all other virtues as being obligatory, only in so far as by reaction and interaction they promote the personal comfort and security of the agent.

The free exercise of benevolence, without regard to the reactive benefits accruing to the agent is, however, *in some sense*, it appears, a moral duty. The duties of the primary morality, Mr. Bain says, are not 'the whole duty of man.' In what sense then, we would ask, is the virtue of benevolence, exercised purely, and without regard to reversions, a moral *duty*? If a moral duty, it must be in some sense obligatory ; and yet we are told (p. 86) that 'actions which people are charged to perform, but are not *punished* for neglecting, may be looked upon as having the *form* of obligation without the reality ;' and (p. 88) that 'actions of pure benevolence do not come within the scope of obligatory duty, but are in a manner left open to the choice of the individual.' '*In a manner*' left open !

And this is all the light that is thrown on the duties of pure Benevolence, of Integrity, Purity, Justice (outside the common law), and so forth. Either these are duties or they are not, either they are obligatory or they are not. If the former, to what or whom are they due, by what law are they enforced? If the latter, why speak of them as moral duties at all, or as moralities in any sense whatsoever?

In the midst of this confusion we turn back again to the Dissertation on ends of human action and find these virtues talked of as 'moral duties strictly so called' (p. 7), and as ends of human action, but 'not equally binding with the primary moral ends,' and again (p. 17), as 'the less imperative duties.' Our confusion is thus increased: they are imperative, and yet not imperative; obligatory, and yet not obligatory.

If this theory of ends and obligations be true of the secondary moralities, in so far as they are not penally enforceable by society, how much more is it applicable to those heroic exhibitions of virtue which belong to what we have termed the tertiary morality. Devotion, self-sacrifice, magnanimity, unbending integrity, heroism, which are the most perfect exhibitions of morality, are not so much moral as artistic, says Mr. Bain, and are 'sought not so much from [their] necessity in human life as from the fascination and charm which they yield to the actor and beholder.' These qualities of character do not come, he says, 'within the scope of the obligatory.' And, in truth, since the virtues, *as such*, are imperative, if at all, in a vague, undefined, and undefinable sense, it would be unreasonable to expect Mr. Bain to allow any obligation to attach to the heroic manifestation of them.

And yet, according to the same author, the nobilities and graces of character, and the virtues as such, are *ends*. We would ask, in what sense can there be for any rational intelligence a true end which is not also *ipso facto*, so far forth, a duty—an obligation? Mr. Bain seems in one passage to see this himself; for, when speaking of Dignity, he says, 'Every creature possesses along with its natural constitution a sense of what that constitution is fit for, and what will put its capacities to the best account; and with this sense there is a *certain feeling* of the high propriety, if not obligation, so to employ itself. As our knowledge of character improves, we are better able to appreciate this fitness, and to feel the corresponding obligation.' After all, then, there is, it seems, a sense of obligation attending even the tertiary morality—the morality of the heroic. If so, how much more must the obligation impose itself on the more moderate exhibitions of the same virtues from all connexion with which it has been excluded!

Until we rid our minds and argument of his overriding theory of obligation, we shall not see our way clearly through the conflicting statements of Mr. Bain. He ought, in the first instance, to have confined himself to *ends*. These once determined, we may obtain some light on the nature of obligation, and, consequently, of the greater or less imperativeness of certain classes of acts. The virtues, in their moderate and heroic form, are in some places admitted by Mr. Bain to be laudable, desirable, and admirable ends of human action. Not only so,—they are, according to him, ends which *transcend* the primary morality, differing from it mainly in this, that they are more than we can fairly ask of men—very much more than we can rightfully *enforce*. But if they are ends, it seems to us that they not only *ought* to be sought after, but because of their transcendent character and their comprehension of all lower moralities, they ought to be *chiefly* sought after. If ends, and therefore duties, in what sense can it be said that they are not obligatory? The apparent self-contradiction arises from a peculiar definition of the word obligatory, as being synonymous with that which can or may be enforced by fines, imprisonments, and corporal inflictions. Had Mr. Bain confined himself in the first instance to ends, apart from the question of obligations, he would have found that every true end of any intelligence is a duty for that intelligence, and that its highest end is its highest duty. In the end itself he would have found the obligation. By these means he would have been led to a definition of obligation which would have shown wherein *primary* obligation consists, and whence it is derived; and he would have found that external penalties and all derivative sanctions are in truth only the secondary and adventitious supports of morality.

If Mr. Bain had with boldness and consistency said, 'There is nothing in the so-called "virtues" or heroisms except a kind of deification of certain words, which, when analysed, reveal nothing but expedients for preserving the individual and the community in security and comfort, and that man has been so constituted that he imagines that he follows after a divine idea when in truth he is only looking after his own security,' his scheme of ethics would at least have had the merit of being scientific. But he does not do so. For, under the name of tenderness, he admits the existence of an innate sentiment of benevolence which has itself for its end. Admitting this, he must also admit those virtues to be ends in themselves into which benevolence enters, such as self-sacrifice, justice, etc. Nor, indeed, can we find that he does not admit this in the case of all virtues which rest on the sentiments. If, therefore, he will only define anew the word Obligation, under the influence of a consideration of all three classes of ethical ends, as laid down by himself, instead of confining himself to the first and lowest, he will find the true source of primary obligation where he will find the ends—namely, in the moral nature of the agent himself. Police ethics will then make way for the ethics of man, and find their true place in the moral code, as the lowest manifestation of those sentiments which constitute the governing elements in human nature, and which cover, on the one hand, the duties which man owes to man, and on the other, those which the individual owes to himself and to God. And when he has thus found in this subjective doctrine a reconciliation of his own contradictory utterances as to ends and obligations, he will have no difficulty in finding, in the same subjective sphere in which he has found ends and primary obligations, a criterion of the right which assigns its true significance to the quantitative morality of utilitarianism, while giving its weight to a loftier scheme of human duty. His ethical vision will take a larger sweep, and not confine itself to those acts which society has a right to control, the consideration of which constitutes a fitting introduction to a treatise on Jurisprudence, but only a small part of Morality.

The fundamental error of Mr. Bain and of all utilitarians is their persistent and exclusive regard to the political side of human actions. Hence their objective treatment of morality as a thing of external ends and external sanctions. They forget the individual moral agent in the needs and well-being of society at large, and thus fix attention on the effect of acts on the common happiness (by which they mean widely diffused comfort and enjoyments) to the exclusion of the character of the *acting*. If they would but consent to individualize their moral speculations, they would discover that what moralists have concern with is the right acting of the individual: that is to say, energizing in accordance with the ultimate ends of man as man; and that the social end falls *within* the larger subjective end as a part of it. The right *social* acting, for example, is that acting which conforms to the sentiments of benevolence and justice, and yields them fruition; the right social *act* is that act which truly attains the external purpose of the sentiment.

Criterion of Rightness.—Our business hitherto has mainly been to allow Mr. Bain to criticise himself, and to justify one of our opening sentences, in which we charge him with having worse confounded the already prevalent confusions of ethical polemics. We have still to inquire into Mr. Bain's criterion of rightness; for although the doctrine of a moral criterion is implicitly contained in the doctrine of moral ends, it is yet necessary to consider these questions apart. We have to look for Mr. Bain's criterion in his chapters on the Moral Sense, and on Obligation. In the former (p. 30) he tells us that the standard or criterion is an *external* one. This it was natural to expect as a consequence from his theory of ends and obligations. That act, he says, is right the whole assignable effects of which on sentient creatures is such as to promote their well-being; and he illustrates this position by the supposed case of discriminate and indiscriminate almsgiving. In the latter case, he says, we have complied with an instinctive morality (which, so far, is not denied), while in the latter we have a morality which commends itself *both* 'to the sentiments and to the reason.' From this we are surely entitled to conclude that there is an inner standard of sentiment which determines the *class* of act which we are to perform, while observation and reason determine the true bearing and ultimate incidence of the act. Suppose the act to be productive of moral or physical harm to the beneficiary, it is wrong; but why? *Because*, we should say, it is thereby shown not to be what it affects to be—a benevolent act. The right thing, after all, then is the conformity of the will with the inner sentiment of benevolence; the individual is right when he conforms to *this*, although he may defeat his moral purpose by inattention to the outer expression of the inner condition of rightness. Conformity with the sentiment might be called the major premiss, of which the minor is the specific act. Had Mr. Bain ignored the sentiments, or denied them, or held to his treatment of them elsewhere[1] as caprices of the individual, vagaries of popular feeling, or irrational impositions of religious teachers, he would not have fallen into the contradictions under which his whole argument labours. He vigorously asserts his utilitarian position with respect to ends, criterion, and obligations; and yet, in every page of his dissertations on Paley, and frequently in his other writings, he inadvertently takes possession of the doctrines of another school, and inserts them in his paragraphs as if they rightfully belonged to his argument. We are thus led into much painful perplexity in any attempt at interpretation. The above mode of putting the utilitarian external standard is an illustration of what we mean. We are told that the criterion of right is *external*, and then, before the paragraph is

[1] *Emotions and the Will*, p. 309, etc.

concluded, we are told that, by looking to the external effects of an act, we satisfy the claims of the *sentiments* as well as of the reason. From which the barest conclusion that can be drawn is that the sentiments are somehow involved in the criterion of the right.

Nor do we find any light thrown on these contradictions by reference to his definition of the opposing *internal* standard against which he argues. There is a cold recklessness in the assertions, that by the internal standard of morality is meant 'the liking or disliking of the individual to the action, apart altogether from its consequences,'[1] and that the utilitarian doctrine 'is a substitution of a regard to consequences for a mere unreasoning sentiment or feeling.'[2] It is scarcely credible that Mr. Bain can have given so little attention to other lines of thought than his own, as to suppose that a subjective moralist inevitably puts the criterion of the right on the individual's 'liking,' and is utterly regardless of the connexion between the right acting and the consequences of his act. There is a school of moralists which maintains that the criterion is to be found in the authoritative utterances of a Moral Sense which has no regard to consequences; but this school is not truly represented except by those who confine the range of this sense to denominations or qualities of acts only. Still less is such a mode of defining the opinions of intuitionalists true of sentimentalists proper. There is no quarrel between them and the utilitarians as to

[1] *Notes on Paley*, p. 36. [2] *Emotions, etc.*, p. 302.

the necessity of tracing acts into their consequences, in order to ascertain whether they truly conform in their final effects to the sentiment from which they sprang. That which we have elsewhere expounded as subjective eudæmonism, points out the true source of the utilitarian error, namely, the non-distinction between the right energizing and the right act which is the effect of that energizing. Let this distinction be preserved, and the question of the nature of the moral act will so far be settled. The quarrel will then be confined to psychological ground, and will be a question as to the nature of these major premisses or sentiments, and the extent to which they are merely self-created means to ends, and in themselves essentially illusory. We shall have to determine whether they are thought-crystallizations of those generalized precepts which tend to the social security, or innate characteristics of all rational intelligences, and therefore ends in themselves—ends of reason, although necessarily having, each according to its nature, a more or less extended history outside itself, which it is our duty to trace and to consider.

In what sense, we would ask, can a thinker maintain the purely external or objective standard to the exclusion of the internal or subjective, who admits into his argument such statements as the following :—' There is [in man] a strong feeling of the rightness of mutually dependent beings acting kindly to each other.'[1] So powerful is this

[1] *Notes on Paley*, p. 38.

feeling or sense, that it 'tends to govern the sense of right.' That is to say, the sense of rightness tends to govern the sense of right! Then he speaks of the 'sense of the beautiful and becoming, as entering into our judgments of right and wrong,' which means, I presume, that the test of the rightness of certain things is their beautifulness and becomingness. Then gratitude, he tells us, is a duty; and why? There are personal and social 'interests' which strengthen its obligation; but, over and above this, we are informed 'that it is called for by an imperious sentiment of *moral fitness and propriety:*' from which it appears that there is a sentiment of moral fitness and propriety which is in some instances a touchstone, test, or standard of the right in conduct. Again, he says, 'The sense of what is for the good of the individual, with reference to the whole compass of being, easily chimes in with the *moral instincts.*' Again, he speaks of the 'elevating and ennobling impulses of our being,' and so forth, until we are utterly at a loss to know on what ground we stand.

Nor are our difficulties removed by finding sentiments talked of as 'certain things founded in taste, liking, aversion, or fancy,' and thus confounded with idiosyncracies and caprices on the one hand, and conventional religious peculiarities on the other.[1] The cup of our surprise is full when we are told (after all that has been said) that ethical inquiry has nothing to do with 'the specific impulses and feelings of human

[1] *Emotions and the Will,* pp. 306-309.

nature that come in to support the maxims of morality.'[1] In other words, the sentimental and emotional side of rational intelligences has nothing to do with the right and obligatory energizing of these intelligences! Such are the consequences of divorcing psychology or the study of mind from the study of the right life of the mind; and of putting forward the duties, which the majority of any community may enforce by penalties, in the name of ethical science properly so called.

To fortify his position against the intuitionalists, Mr. Bain looks into history, and finds revealed '*in the process of the enactment of moral rules*' the true source of moral precepts and practices, and, by consequence, the *real* standard to which intuitionalists daily refer when they fancy they are appealing to an inner discriminating Sense and authoritative law.[2] A Solon, a Lycurgus, a Mahomet, a George Fox, or the State represented by some one individual clothed with legislative authority, prescribe certain rules of conduct which their followers or subjects accept and practice, not as in themselves right, but through blind faith in the utterer. But, we ask, by what means do these men themselves reach their rules? and the answer must be, by reflection on the constitution and destiny of man. Rules and maxims belong to the secondary or derivative morality, and rest for their validity on their harmony with the universal nature of man. The framer of them believes that he is constructing pre-

---

[1] *Notes on Paley*, p. 92.   [2] *Emotions, etc.*, pp. 311, 312.

cepts which do so harmonize and which will best secure for man the highest good possible for him here and hereafter. Followers of the more thoughtful kind accept these maxims, because they themselves discern this harmony and fitness, while many, doubtless, are led by ulterior ends or sinister motives, and not a few by the felt need of some law or other as a controlling power in communities. To stop short at the secondary or preceptive morality is to stop at the threshold of the inquiry. It is this very secondary morality as uttered by the legislator or prophet, or by a more powerful than either, King Nomos, which is itself the subject of inquiry and of controversy. When a schoolmaster prescribes certain bounds beyond which his boys are not to wander, is the precept founded on the arbitrary will of the master?

We are told, in illustration of the revolutions possible in morality, of the change of feeling in the United States on the subject of slavery. An abhorrence of slaveholding now exists which two centuries ago was not known. And were the anti-slavery party now to succeed in making the maintenance of their opinions a 'term of communion,' the abhorrence would be developed into a 'moral sentiment.' There is here a confounding of sentiments with maxims professedly based on sentiment, and an implied attempt to convey that all 'moral sentiments' are artificial notions of the human mind which may be made to order. That man would be a fool who did not admit that the bearing of the sentiments on our social relations, on custom, laws, and on our own personal conduct, is capable from age to age of larger interpretation and of greater refinement and of ever-increasing complexity. The constitution of human nature, and the fact of the existence of the sentiments as motives and ends, and *therefore* obligations, remains, notwithstanding, unchanged. We deny then that it is 'mere trifling to fill our imagination with [what Mr. Bain calls] an unseen, unproducible standard of morality;' nor do we think that Solon, Mahomet, and other leaders of men were, taken severally or conjointly, the authority that 'originally prescribed almost any moral precept now recognised as binding.' It might surely have occurred to Mr. Bain that to imagine that intuitionalism, maintained in one form or another as it has been by the weightiest intellects of Europe, was convertible with a kind of bastard-Hobbism, was either 'trifling' with his subject, or utterly misconceiving it.

Moral Sense.—Like many others, Mr. Bain, in his remarks on the Moral Sense or Conscience—terms which he regards as equivalent—unwittingly confounds the Derivative Conscience with the primary discriminating instinct of rightness. The former is that aggregation of precepts, rules, sentiments, and feelings of obligation which every man trained in a civilized community carries about with him, and from out of which he draws from day to day and hour to hour the moral weapons which the occasions of life require. The latter is that power or process whereby a man originally discerns the right act from the wrong. The Derivative Conscience all men are at one about: they differ as to the mode of its formation, and the primitive elements which enter into the composite structure.

It is true that those who maintain the existence in man of a distinct Faculty or Sense which, in every particular case, unreasoningly and unerringly selects from out of a number of possible individual acts that act which is alone *right*, identify the primary and the derivative conscience. But what thinker (save Warburton and, in a distant degree, Butler) can be said to do this? Conscience in this sense is the conscience of the vulgar, and of necessity the conscience of oratory; but it finds no place in the creed of (at least) any recent philosophy. And yet it is against the Moral Sense so conceived that Mr. Bain and his school generally direct their attacks, and it is over this that they celebrate an easy victory. Our business is with a certain power, capacity, instinct, or sense in man which *discriminates*—as an act of judgment of course, for this form all conscious movements of a rational being must take—certain governing motives of conduct from one another and *forces* the affirmation of rightness regarding the one and wrongness regarding the other. But we shall not here enter further into the general question, but confine ourselves, as we have done hitherto, to Mr. Bain's own reasonings, and to the exhibition of their inherent contradictoriness.

We might of course expect that Mr. Bain, having adopted the external standard of rightness, would deny an innate faculty of moral discrimination; for, if the standard be external, and, as he says, 'exposed to the observation and understanding of all men,' the faculties of observation, comparison, and inference are adequate to the function of moral discrimination and moral direction. To look for any fresh power or sense would be to run counter to one of the first principles of philosophical inquiry. But after he has taken up this position, we are surprised to find him defining the 'Moral Sense'[1] and the 'Conscience' as the feeling or faculty of approval and disapproval. Is then the affirmation of approval a *different* process psychologically from the affirmation that two and two make four; and is the affirmation of disapproval a different psychological process from the affirmation that six times six are *not* thirty-seven? If some hidden element enters into the one judgment which does not enter into the other, what is that element?

For our part, we should have expected a more thorough and consistent treatment of these important terms. Mr. Bain ought, feeling how pertinaciously they cling even to his own thought, to have felt also how they secretly vitiated his conclusions, and to have got rid of them once and for all in some such way as this: The Moral Sense or Conscience is vulgarly held to be a feeling of approbation and disapprobation, and by these words a moral judg-

[1] *Emotions and the Will*, pp. 286 and 297.

ment is usually distinguished from an intellectual judgment. But if we admit this separation of terms in speaking of a specific class of phenomena, we *ipso facto* admit the stirring up of something in us on the presentation of certain acts, which is more than the intellectual affirmation of the fitness of certain movements to attain certain external results—something emotional, and pleasurable, and law-giving: we therefore discard the terms as illusory, and as wrongfully usurping a place which rightfully belongs to the words 'fitness and unfitness.'

Having abjured a Moral Sense, our author then sets about showing how the characteristics of the so-called Moral Sense or Conscience may be accounted for without having recourse to a separate faculty or feeling.[1] But here again his argument, in so far as it is good, is good only against the vulgar theory of a Conscience as the arbitrary discriminator and dictator of the right and the wrong in each particular act. We are entitled, however, to assume that he is endeavouring to make good his point against intuitionalism generally. This he is far from doing: his reasoning is powerless against the doctrine which, we believe, really underlies the vulgar one, and which we have endeavoured elsewhere to disentomb; that, namely, which maintains the existence of certain innate feelings called sentiments, by which we measure acts, and which are ends in themselves, though not *fulfilling* themselves in themselves. In opposition to this subjective sentimental theory all utilitarian attempts to construct a

[1] *Notes on Paley*, p. 37.

non-sentimental theory of discrimination, dictation, and approbation inevitably break down. Mr. Bain himself tells us, in his attempt to construct the conscience, that 'there is a strong *feeling* of the *rightness* of mutually dependent beings acting kindly to each other' . . . that 'a Conscience without a heart would not come up to the Conscience either of the moralist or of the multitude' . . . and again, that 'the same power that enables a man to arrive at truth gives the perception of truth, and with that perception, all the approbation and satisfaction that the adherence to truth can inspire;' from which it would appear that there is an intellectual approbation of truthfulness or integrity capable of being stirred into pleasurable emotion irrespectively of consequences. Nor is this all; for, according to our author himself, 'we must include the *feeling* of *what is beautiful and noble* among the conspiring ingredients of the moral sense of the generality of mankind;' from which it follows, that there is a feeling or sentiment of the beautiful in conduct, which can be stirred into pleasurable emotion on the perception by the intellect of certain acts, and which, therefore, is an end in itself and for itself. There is also, we are told, 'an *imperious* sentiment of moral fitness and propriety altogether apart (in the case of gratitude, and therefore in other cases) from the consideration of justice, or of the evil consequences to society, of discouraging the authors of benefits;' and so on. But if these sentiments are ends, they are also obligations. It accordingly becomes as impossible to extract consistency out of such heterogeneous statements regarding a Moral Sense, as we have found it to be to harmonize Mr. Bain's expositions of ends, criterion, and obligation.

So much for the Conscience or Moral Sense as a discriminator and approver. The mixing up of the two functions is not our fault. There is a third function, that of an authority, a law, a binding force. On pages 286 and 297 of the *Emotions and the Will*, Mr. Bain defines Conscience (which he identifies with the Moral Sense) as *the feeling of approbation and reprobation*. On page 313, when he again has to treat of the same subject, he, without notice of the separate moral functions which enter into the complex notion, treats of Conscience as meaning a sentiment of authority or duty. In this confounding of the functions of that which is popularly and indefinitely called 'Conscience,' Mr. Bain has so many companions, both of the utilitarian and the intuitive school, that we do no more than make this passing allusion to it as a common source of error. It of course follows, from the fact that all obligation proceeds *from without*, that Conscience, as an obligatory sentiment, is simply an artificial image in the mind of external authority—'an imitation within ourselves of the government without us.' No objection can be taken to this description of the genesis of the human Conscience which has not been already taken to the theory of obligation itself. If there be no inner obligatory forces penal and recompensing, there is then no such thing as an inner Conscience save as an illusion of the imagination or the intellect. And there is nothing more to be said about it.

The history which Mr. Bain gives of the growth of the sense of obligation or duty in the human mind, from childhood upwards, is interesting and valuable, in so far as external forces are concerned. We do not think, however, that it is strictly accurate, except where the early training of children is based on deterrent influences. Not terror, as Mr. Bain maintains, but *force as such*, is the first great lesson of childhood—force resisting the spontaneous movements of the body and the will of the child, but not necessarily associated with pain and fear. To this succeeds the *anticipation* of force as a preventive of certain acts, but not as a deterrent in the sense of stirring up fear. We cannot therefore admit, as the result of our observation, that 'the infant conscience is nothing but the linking of terror with forbidden actions.' The deterrent influences, doubtless, come in to support the others sooner or later, and continue throughout life increasing rather than decreasing in power as the knowledge of life extends.

We notice that Mr. Bain gives to the approbation of others *as such*, apart from the consequences of it, an importance and an *external* power of an obligatory character which is denied to it elsewhere, but which, if fully accorded, might prepare the way for a new casting of the chapters on ends and obligations, which would lift his moral theory altogether out of the utilitarian rut.

We might point to further inconsistencies of statement arising from unconscious appropriations of non-utilitarian doctrines, to which Mr. Bain is driven by a necessity similar to that which we have already seen operating in other parts of his argument. This, however, would involve repetition and might be superfluous. But after having followed him through the windings and inconsistencies of his theoretical exposition, we cannot read his concluding remarks without respect for his loyalty to party at least, and to the thesis he had to maintain, qualified though that respect be by the pertinacity of his misconceptions and the negligence of his logic. He concludes by telling us now, as at first, that 'positive beneficence,' 'good offices,' 'positive good deeds,' 'self-sacrifice,' are 'not objects of moral approbation;' that they are objects of 'esteem and reward,' but 'transcend the region of morality proper!' If they are not moral, not approvable, not right, not obligatory, what are they, and what new vocabulary shall we teach our children? After all that has been said, does it come to this, that Mr. Bain has only got this familiar lesson of Jurisprudence to teach us, that duties which the State enforces by penalties have a larger *quantitative* sanction than those which are the fruit of a free and spontaneous development of our rational nature in harmony with its lofty aims and great destiny?

EDINBURGH: T. CONSTABLE,
PRINTER TO THE QUEEN, AND TO THE UNIVERSITY.

BY THE SAME AUTHOR.

On the Philosophy of Ethics:
An Analytical Essay.

PRICE 6s.

On the Fundamental Doctrine of
Latin Syntax.

PRICE 5s.

Primary Instruction in Relation
to Education.

PRICE 4s. 6d.

www.ingramcontent.com/pod-product-compliance
Lightning Source LLC
Chambersburg PA
CBHW030257170426
43202CB00009B/780